D0402199

HIDDEN
IN PLAIN SIGHT

A Practical Guide to Concealed Handgun Carry

TREY BLOODWORTH
MIKE RALEY

Photographs by Mike Raley and Guy Griswold

Library of Congress Catalog 95–69836

ISBN 1–57087–168–X

Professional Press
Chapel Hill, NC 27515-4371

Manufactured in the United States of America

98 97 96 95   10 9 8 7 6 5 4 3 2 1

CONTENTS

Introduction   vii

General Concealed Carry   1

Belt Holsters   13

Shoulder, Ankle
and Pocket Holsters   41

Accessory Holsters   59

Miscellaneous Concealed
Carry Holsters   71

Concealed Carry Holsters
for Women   87

Access Times of Various
Concealed Carry Modes   101

Conclusion   107

Bibliography   113

Appendix   115

ACKNOWLEDGEMENTS

Special thanks to: Connie, Debi, Ma & Pa, Jack, Mike, Elaine, Mark, Guy and Darrell.

Also, we are forever indebted to the founding fathers of this great country who had the foresight to protect our right to keep and bear arms in the Constitution of the United States of America.

INTRODUCTION

This book is about legal, effective concealed handgun carry. It is not a book on gun fighting tactics, handgun caliber selection or combat shooting. While volumes have been written on these worthy topics, only limited and piecemeal information has been available about concealed carry techniques. It is amazing that so many people will spend an enormous amount of time selecting the "perfect" carry gun and ammunition, yet put little thought or money into their holster. The end result is that because of uncomfortable or inadequate holsters, handguns that were purchased as carry guns get left in a drawer. Remember, the first rule of gun fighting is to bring a gun! Whether you are a new CCW (concealed carry weapon) permit holder, or someone who's been "carrying" for years, this book will help when you are choosing your equipment.

Choosing the correct concealment holster can be a daunting task. There are literally dozens of styles available, most of which are not available at the local discount store, gun shop or even gun show. While you could spend hundreds of dollars and months of frustration buying and experimenting with various concealment holsters, this book will help you identify the best options in advance. This book presents honest, unbiased opinions on the products discussed. Unlike some gun-related magazines, whose publishers choose to keep their advertisers happy with positive product reviews, this book will point out equipment that is below par. Special emphasis will be placed on how to dress for effective concealed carry, as well as how the various carry modes rank in terms of accessibility. The last chapter covers the CCW mindset and accompanying responsibilities. Finally, the Appendix offers an extensive list of sources for holsters and CCW accessories.

Since you are reading this book, you are obviously concerned about your own security and/or the security of loved ones. You realize that even though police officers are heroically battling violent crime (with minimal pay), chances are that you will be forced to protect yourself if violently attacked. The math is simple - the police simply cannot be there for everyone all of the time. In addition, many U.S. courts have ruled that the police are not responsible for protecting individuals; most conclude that the police are bound to uphold the law and protect the community in general (Warren v. District of Columbia, etc.). The brutal truth is that you are ultimately responsible for your own protection. Without a gun, a small man or woman cannot be expected to stop a 200+ pound violent attacker, regardless of the amount of self-defense training the individual has had. Popular wisdom notwithstanding, methods such as kicking the assailant "where the sun doesn't shine" or defending yourself with an umbrella or police whistle are just as ineffective as they sound. The chances are that none of these simplistic "defenses" will halt a determined assailant. However, a CCW helps tip the scales in the victim's favor. An adequately powered handgun in the hands of a well-trained individual can level the playing field like nothing else. Because of this, women especially should consider the option of a CCW, and this book contains a chapter devoted to the concealed carry needs of women.

The reality that self protection is primarily the responsibility of the individual is one of the reasons that the founding fathers of this country included in the Bill of Rights an amendment that reaffirms the inalienable right of the people to "keep and bear arms". The fact that this statement is in the Bill of Rights instead of the Constitution itself shows that the framers of the Constitution believed that the "right to keep and bear arms" was a right that predated the Constitution; not a right granted by it. While this is the case with all of the first ten amendments, most liberals vehemently support the Bill of Rights with the exception of the second amendment. (Question - How does the ACLU count to ten? Answer - One, three, four five...) Gun-grabbers are appalled by the second amendment because they know that their dream of wholesale "gun control" is patently unconstitutional. This is covered in detail in the essay "The Embarrassing Second Amendment" by law Professor Sanford Levinson. Mr. Levinson, who supports "gun control," nevertheless draws the conclusion that banning private gun ownership from qualified citizens is unconstitutional. He hypothesizes that "gun control" has made it thus far because most lawyers and judges are liberal and support "gun control"; otherwise it would have been declared unconstitutional long ago. (As an aside - "Gun control" is in quotes because true gun control is an effective grip, sight alignment and trigger squeeze that results in hitting your intended target.)

The random violence that has become commonplace is another reason that many people are increasingly concerned about personal security. It is no longer enough to "mind your own business" to avoid trouble. This perception is supported by the FBI's report "Crime in the United States - 1993," that was released in December of 1994. This report states that in America today, you are more likely to be murdered by a stranger than ever before (as opposed to being murdered by someone you know.) Consider the following quotes from the "Homicide Patterns" section of this report:

> When addressing victim/offender relationships, murders by strangers and unknown persons represented 53 percent of the murders in the Nation during 1992. This percentage represents a historical high. (p. 283)

> The typical assumptions associated with homicides throughout this century must be reevaluated in view of the unprecedented shift in national homicide patterns as evidenced during the 1990s. Every American now has a realistic chance of murder victimization in view of the random nature the crime has assumed. This notion is somewhat supported by the fact that a majority of the Nation's murder victims are now killed by strangers or unknown persons. (pp. 286-287)

Because of this increase in random murders, more people than ever are exploring the option of carrying a concealed handgun for personal defense.

There are many reasons for carrying handguns concealed versus exposed, ranging from the tactical to the legal. One of the biggest advantages of a concealed carry weapon (CCW) is the element of surprise. There is also a certain social stigma associated with going to a theater or restaurant with an exposed handgun strapped on your side. Said exposed handgun could also make you the first target of someone with criminal (or bullying) intentions. Another advantage of concealed carry is that bad guys don't know who's carrying, so EVERYONE might be. This increases the deterrent effect of concealed versus open carry. Unfortunately, in many states it is illegal to carry a concealed weapon. In this case, some people may decide that the threat of violent attack outweighs the danger of being charged with a concealed weapons violation. Many subscribe to the wisdom in the old quote, "I'd rather be tried by twelve than carried by six." For this reason an honest, otherwise law-abiding citizen may consider it necessary to carry his handgun extremely well concealed to keep from being arrested and booked as a criminal himself! Thankfully, a growing number of states (including recently Utah, Virginia and Arkansas) are reforming their laws and offering CCW permits to all qualified citizens.

Some critics may say that a book about effective concealed handgun carry can be used by the criminal element as well as by law-abiding citizens. However, potential criminals are deterred by armed "victims." Prison interviews with convicted felons support the deterrent effect that armed citizens have on crime. In 1985, two University of Massachusetts professors, James D. Wright and Peter H. Rossi, conducted an in-depth study that included interviews with 1,874 felons in ten states. This study, "The Armed Criminal in America: A Survey of Incarcerated Felons," was commissioned by the National Institute of Justice (NIJ). Two consistent opinions that the felons shared were: 1) an armed citizen is clearly a deterrent to a criminal , and 2) most criminals would rather run into a cop than an armed "victim."

Many of the examples that gun-grabbers use to argue for tougher gun control laws can also be used to argue for expanded concealed carry rights. They are notorious for using mass-murder cases as examples of why tougher gun control laws are needed. They conveniently ignore the fact that the killers violated all sorts of other laws (like laws against murder), which suggests that the killers will ignore the new gun control laws as well. In reality, these examples often illustrate why concealed carry rights need to be expanded. One competent person with a CCW on the Long Island Railroad with Colin Ferguson could have possibly prevented, or at least reduced the magnitude of that tragedy. Likewise, according to her 1993 testimony given before the Texas House Public Safety Committee, Dr. Suzanna Gratia potentially could have prevented the massacre at Luby's Cafeteria in Kileen, Texas had she not quit carrying her .38 revolver in her purse because she feared that she was in violation of Texas' concealed weapons law. When the Kileen incident was over, 23 people were dead, including Gratia's parents. Thousands of other tragedies are prevented every year by law abiding citizens using firearms in self-defense. According to Florida State University Professor Gary Kleck, guns were used defensively between 606,000 and 960,000 times each year between 1976 and 1990 (excluding police and military uses.) Dr. Kleck says that the defender actually fired the gun in fewer than one out of four cases; the mere presence of the defensive gun was deterrent enough in the remaining three-fourths of the cases. Another statistic noted by Dr. Kleck is that only 12.1% of people who resisted an assault with a gun suffered injury. This compares to 29.5% of the people who fought back with a knife, 52.1% who resisted with their bare hands and 27.3% of those who did not offer any resistance. If the people who used a gun to resist assault had all been properly trained, the percentage who were injured would have probably been even lower. These statistics are available in Dr. Kleck's book, *Point Blank: Guns and Violence in America.*

Whether or not to be armed for self-defense is an intensely personal choice. However, the forces of the anti-self-defense lobby are working hard to make that choice for you. Because of this, it is imperative for law-abiding citizens to make their voices heard on this issue. Let your representatives in Washington know that you do not support attacks on the Bill of Rights and on the right to self-defense. Also, if you are not a member of the NRA or another gun rights group, consider joining. It is a small price to pay to protect one of our most precious freedoms.

Warning! Check your state and local laws before carrying a handgun, concealed or otherwise. Laws vary widely from place to place. Some states allow concealed carry without a permit, some require a permit and some states do not allow concealed handgun carry at all. All states put restrictions on where guns can be legally carried. In addition, several states outlaw particular modes of concealed carry. Your local police department or District Attorney's office should know the details.

Chapter 1
GENERAL CONCEALED CARRY

This chapter will cover some of the basics of concealed carry. Contrary to popular belief, you do not have to dress and look like a Secret Service agent to be able to effectively conceal a handgun. However, you will probably need to make some adjustments to your wardrobe. While it is possible to conceal a full-sized handgun on most people, it cannot be accomplished without some effort. The wide selection of excellent holsters that has evolved over the last few years makes concealed carry easier than ever. There are no hard and fast rules about concealed carry for all people; concealed carry must be tailored to the individual.

Choosing a Concealed Carry Weapon
I would like to briefly discuss handgun selection. There are several good rules of thumb to follow. To paraphrase a noted combat handgun guru concerning lethal confrontation, you want to "get there first with the most." This can be translated into choosing the largest caliber that you can competently handle. A solid hit with a .38 Special is better than a miss with a .45 ACP. You will be better off with a lesser caliber that you enjoy shooting enough to practice with regularly than with a massive caliber with which you refuse to practice (or cannot afford to practice.)

A good reference for choosing your caliber is Marshall's and Sanow's *Handgun Stopping Power*. This informative book was published in 1992 and is a compilation of the results of over 7000 actual shootings. The original research for the book was Marshall's quest for the superior "one shot stop" cartridge. Controversial and myth-shattering, this book has a wealth of excellent "street data."

Shot placement is much more critical than caliber, so choose a caliber with which you are comfortable and accurate with and practice, practice, practice! Not only should you practice general marksmanship, but you should practice drawing from concealment. This should first be practiced extensively with an unloaded gun and only after it has been mastered and with safety foremost in mind should you practice with live rounds. Carrying a concealed handgun and not practicing from a draw is like planning to compete in the Daytona 500 without ever getting your race car on a racetrack.

The choice of a handgun suitable for daily use will vary widely from person to person. In the book *Blue Steel and Gunleather*, holster designer and concealed carry expert John Bianchi explains "Bianchi's Law" which he describes as "A one gun, one carry dictum": "While many different combinations of holster and gun are available, there will be one that is just right for each individual, considering body height and weight." Mr. Bianchi believes that a person should not deviate from this combination once he has discovered it. If you can follow this principle, then by all means do so. The advantage of one gun and one mode of carry is that you can focus your finite training time on just one mode of carry versus dividing your training time among various modes of carry. Theoretically, with enough practice from one carry mode, drawing the gun and firing should become an instinctive reaction that will not fail you in times of stress. This is the ideal situation: to always be able to carry the same gun in the same holster. Following this dictum is tactically superior to using various modes of concealed carry, though it may not always be practical. This "one gun rule" would be great if we all lived in a perfect world where it never got over 75 degrees Fahrenheit and sports coats were perennially fashionable, even for yard work! Alas, this is not the case, so the concept of different guns for different "niches" is actually practical, if you can afford it. Still, for most people, one CCW can be sufficient if chosen carefully.

It cannot be stressed enough that in choosing a carry gun, you must *select one that you will be able to carry and conceal regularly.* Some macho men proclaim, "I'll carry my Government model .45 or nothing - No mouse guns for me!" While this indeed sounds manly, it is not always practical. If these same "tough guys" were surveyed, the results would show that most of them do not regularly carry their .45's. Remember from the introduction that the first rule of gun fighting is to bring a gun! (This also happens to be the first rule of knife fighting.) In a lethal confrontation, the .380 that you brought with you is much more useful than the .45 that you left at home.

Concealed carry of a handgun should be a happy balance of concealment, power (caliber), capacity, access and comfort. Several factors must be considered when choosing a CCW: body type (or frame size), weather/environment/location, experience, gender, and hand strength/dexterity. A concealed carry handgun and holster must be specifically chosen for the person who will carry it; there is no "one size fits all." Larger framed people generally have an easier time concealing a handgun than smaller framed people, but this simply means that slightly built people must be more resourceful in selecting their carry mode. It is typically easier to hide a CCW in cool weather, where people wear more layers of clothing, so the temperature is definitely a consideration. By the same token, a CCW on the beach presents other unique challenges. Gender is a factor because women have the advantage of myriad holster purses that can superbly conceal nearly any size handgun. I suppose that men could use these purses as well, but not as inconspicuously. On the other hand, current fashion is often less forgiving of baggy clothes on women, and the typical female frame is smaller than that of the typical male. Finally, hand strength and dexterity are factors because different handguns require varying amounts of strength and dexterity for trigger, slide, safety and magazine manipulation. For example, if one has lost hand strength or mobility due to arthritis or some other ailment, this is a significant variable that must be considered before purchasing a CCW.

One decision relevant to concealed carry is whether to buy a revolver or semiautomatic. Revolvers, of course, hold their ammunition in a rotating cylinder. This cylinder tends to be rather thick, limiting the concealability of the gun in some carry modes. Semi-autos (or just "autos") are usually thinner and are an attractive concealed carry option when handgun thickness is critical. However, an auto's grip is frequently larger than that of a revolver, reducing its concealability for certain carry modes. In general, less experienced gunowners prefer revolvers over semiautomatics for two reasons: revolvers are simpler to use and they have a reputation for being more reliable than autos. This does not mean that many experts do not use revolvers - they do, and for the same reasons. Well-built and maintained autoloaders can be extremely reliable, but poorly maintained autos are much less forgiving than poorly maintained revolvers.

The handgun's method of operation is also something to consider when shopping for a concealable handgun. "Single-action" (SA) means that the hammer must be manually cocked before the gun can be fired. SA revolvers require far too much practice to be a practical defense option for most people, while SA autos are enormously popular for self-defense. SA autos are typically cocked by racking the slide to load a round from the magazine into the chamber. Many SA autos are designed to be carried with the hammer cocked and the safety on, commonly called "Condition One" or "cocked and locked." Some SA auto manufacturers advise against carrying their SA autos in Condition One. These manufacturers usually advocate "Condition Two" - hammer down on a loaded chamber (or hammer half-cocked on a loaded chamber). A few advocate "Condition Three" - hammer down on an empty chamber. If the auto is to be carried in a purse or pocket, it may be difficult to safely cock the handgun if it is in Condition Two, or to chamber a round in Condition Three without removing the gun from the purse or pocket. If you choose a SA auto for defense, one that is designed to be carried in Condition One will be your best bet. "Double-action" (DA) handguns can be cocked manually and then fired single-action, or can be fired by squeezing the trigger with the hammer down - in which case the hammer is cocked by the trigger pull. Most suitable defense revolvers can be fired double-action, and that is how the bulk of self-defense practice should be done with these handguns. DA autos are also fine for defense, and like their SA brethren they will be cocked for subsequent shots by the cycling of the slide. However, DA autos are usually slightly larger than their SA counterparts. "Double-action-only" (DAO) handguns eliminate the option of manually cocking the hammer, and force the shooter to use the long pull of a double-action trigger for every shot. Because DAO revolvers have internal or spurless hammers, they are an excellent choice for pocket or purse carry, as they can be fired repeatedly without being drawn. DAO autos may also have internal hammers, but a DAO auto (or auto of any type) can typically be fired only once from inside a pocket or purse since the gun is almost certain to jam as the action cycles or the spent casing is ejected. Another factor - since the hammer is already cocked on SA handguns, they typically have a lighter trigger pull than other actions. Most people feel that a lighter trigger pull is conducive to accurate shooting. Many people have difficulty adjusting to rapid second shots of a DA auto since they are single-action and have a significantly lighter trigger pull than the first double-action shot had.

The choice of grips on your gun is important for effective concealed carry. Guns with rounded "butts" (the base of the grip) are less likely to be visible under an untucked shirt than guns with square butts, because there is no distinct edge for your shirt to fold over. Rounded butt replacement grips for most common revolvers are readily available from Hogue, Pachmayr, Eagle, and others. Another factor to consider is the material from which the grip is made. Soft rubber grips can aid in reducing felt recoil, but they have a tendency to snag or "hang up" on concealing fabric. This can slow access to the gun, especially if the gun is carried in a pocket. Rubber grips can also pose concealment problems. For instance, if your gun is worn beneath an untucked shirt, the shirt will not slide easily across the gun as you bend and move. For these situations, wood or plastic grips are a better choice. Grip selection is of less concern for users of shoulder holsters.

Another issue often overlooked when purchasing a gun for concealed carry is the style of hammer and sights used on the gun. Some guns are produced without the traditional hammer "spur" to provide two benefits. First, a shielded or internal hammer is less likely to snag on the draw. This is especially beneficial for purse or pocket carry. Secondly, a shielded/internal hammer is designed so that it is difficult or impossible to get clothing between the hammer and the firing pin, thus making pocket-firing more reliable, especially with revolvers. As with hammers, overly large sights can cause the gun to snag on the draw. This is a reason that many people eschew large adjustable sights on defense guns, instead choosing models with low-profile fixed sights.

There is an additional factor to consider when choosing a CCW. The more popular or common the handgun that you select, the wider range of holster choices you will have. The more expensive custom holster shops can build a good holster for virtually any gun, but you pay for this custom work. The less expensive mass produced holsters and accessories are made primarily for the more popular handguns. A good example is the "Firestar," manufactured by Eibar Star of Spain. The "Firestar M-40" is an excellent compact semi-automatic in .40 S&W caliber, but holsters for this gun were hard to come by until recently. I bought an M-40 several years ago and was very pleased with the gun, but the mass produced holster options were limited. DeSantis was the first major holster manufacturer I discovered that offered carry rigs specifically molded for the Firestar. Before I learned that DeSantis offered holsters for this gun, I was nearly resigned to purchasing a custom built holster at a premium price simply because the Firestar was not yet widely popular. After the Firestar won the 1993 "Handgun of the Year Award," the less expensive holster options were greatly expanded. The moral of the story is to make sure that a good selection of holsters is available for the model gun you are interested in before you purchase your CCW. A more recent example is the Makarov - These guns are selling like proverbial hotcakes, but concealment holsters for them are still scarce.

One way to minimize cost when selecting a CCW and holster combination is to consider your summer attire. If you are financially restricted to one CCW and holster, determine what combination you would be able to carry in the summer. Make a note of the types of clothes that you wear in the summer as well as the types of summer activities in which you participate. It is generally more difficult to effectively conceal a handgun in the summer, so if you choose a rig that you can conceal in the summer, it will be relatively easy to conceal it in cooler weather. If you are not financially limited, you may be able to purchase additional holsters or handguns that may be more comfortable or convenient for cool weather wear, but the summer rig is the minimum combination that you can get by with for all seasons. Another way to reduce expensive experimentation is to borrow different types of holsters from friends. If this is an option, you may be able to wear different combinations to see what works best for you.

Confidence

When you carry a concealed handgun it is critical that you are confident, both of your ability and the concealment of your gun. If you are nervous about either, it will be obvious to those around you. One habit that professionals notice when looking for concealed weapons is the tendency of the carrier to unconsciously touch or feel for his weapon. This is the same method some pickpockets use to spot people carrying a large sum of money or other valuables. Many people want to touch their gun or money to be reassured that it is still in place. (Another method professionals use is to watch what people do when it suddenly starts raining. As people with concealed handguns run for shelter, they have a tendency to grab and hold their concealed gun securely to their body. This is a dead giveaway.) You must be comfortable enough with your CCW so that this confirmation is not necessary. Develop this confidence by wearing your CCW around your home until it becomes natural to you. The intent is not to forget that it is there, but rather to become confident that you can effectively wear it concealed. Another crucial confidence builder is to have a friend or spouse "look" for your CCW before you venture into public with it. If you have told someone that you are wearing a handgun and they still cannot find it, this is a huge confidence booster. However, do not expect this confidence to come overnight. It takes many long days of wearing your CCW to reduce your self-consciousness. The first several times that you wear your concealed carry gun in public you will feel as if everyone is staring at you (or your gun). This is natural. It will take time to become accustomed to the new weight on your hip (or under your shoulder, in your purse, etc.). Some self-consciousness is to your advantage; the quickest way to expose your CCW is to become too nonchalant about regularly carrying a handgun. Also, I have found that a quality holster inspires confidence, while a poorly designed holster causes uncertainty.

Weight Distribution

Weight distribution is included in this chapter about general concealed carry because it applies to all modes of concealed carry. If you are carrying more weight on one side of your body than the other, this may be noticeable in your gait. For example, if you are carrying a large, heavy pistol on your right side, you will unconsciously swing your left arm slightly more than your right arm when you walk. This is a natural act that your body performs to maintain proper balance. Even beyond the change in your stride, uneven weight distribution can make you feel as if you are listing to one side. One way to avoid this phenomenon is to balance the weight of your gun. This may be done with spare magazines or speed loaders, or by rearranging the items that you normally carry on your person. If you carry your gun on your strong side, you may carry your wallet, keys, loose change and pocketknife on your weak side to balance the weight of your gun.

Holster Material

What is the best holster material available? Leather, ballistic nylon, polymer, composite or some type of fabric? Horsehide or cowhide leather? There is no single answer but this: the optimum material for a holster is the material that best meets your individual requirements. Leather is a good holster material, but leather does not hold up as well in a jungle as some of the new polymer and ballistic nylon holsters. Leather holsters can be made with such a good fit that a thumb break or other retaining device is unnecessary. Leather holsters do not have the tendency to be as noisy or to "rustle" like ballistic nylon holsters. (Still, if a leather belt holster is worn on a belt that does not properly fit, it can "creak" or "squeak".) However, holsters made of ballistic nylon are often substantially cheaper than leather, and this may be the deciding factor for some people. Some nylon holsters are designed to fit several different guns of similar size because they are not molded for a specific gun. The disadvantage of these is the poor fit; some restraining device will be needed to retain the handgun in the holster. Some of the synthetic materials like the polymers and composites are more resistant to water and heat, but this varies depending on the material. You often hear, incorrectly, that "a good leather holster will last a lifetime." No holster will last a lifetime if it is worn every day; any material will eventually wear out if used enough. Still, a well built leather or synthetic holster will give you many years of service if cared for properly. Personally, I still prefer leather for my carry rigs. If I were in a rain forest I would choose a synthetic, but I find the aesthetic appeal of top-grain leather irresistible. A last note about materials; it is probably not a good idea to store a gun in a leather holster over the long-term. The materials used in the leathers of some suppliers can cause corrosion problems to the finish on many guns.

Clothing

Dressing for a CCW is not as difficult as you might think. Your wardrobe should depend on the mode of carry that you employ. Still, some basic rules apply to all concealed carry. Dark colors generally "print" a gun less than light colors do, as do clothes with a "busy" pattern. ("Printing" occurs when the outline of the gun is visible through the concealing garment.) Similarly, heavier or thicker fabrics hide a gun better than thinner materials. Do not wear something that is grossly out of season, because the last thing you want to do is stand out from the crowd. The ever popular safari/photojournalist vests offer perfect concealment for most belt holsters, but in many urban areas of the country they are as obvious as a sign that says, "I'm definitely wearing a gun, and I'm probably an off duty police officer." Noted gun writer Jan Libourel has commented that if he were a felon leaving a crime, he would shoot everyone in sight that was wearing one of these photojournalist vests under the assumption that they were armed!

In the next several chapters I will discuss various concealed carry options, ranging from the traditional to the exotic. There are several questions to keep in mind as you decide what will work best for you. How will this carry mode fit into my lifestyle? How accessible is the gun in this mode? How comfortable is this mode? And, most importantly, will I actually use this mode on a regular basis? More holster-specific clothing considerations will be discussed as the various types of holsters are covered in the following chapters.

Chapter 2
BELT HOLSTERS

Belt holsters are the most traditional holsters for hand guns, and when most people think of a holster the image of a belt holster usually springs to mind (unless they've been watching too many reruns of "Miami Vice"). However, some of today's belt holsters are anything but traditional, and the many types of belt holsters can be confusing to the first-time buyer. Belt holsters can be broken down into two basic categories: those that are worn inside the pants and those that are worn outside of the pants. Inside the pants holsters are also commonly referred to as inside-the-waistband holsters or IWB holsters. As a general rule, IWB holsters are more easily concealed than outside-the-pants belt holsters. IWB holsters can often be concealed simply with an untucked shirt, while other belt holsters usually require a jacket or vest for effective concealment. Some IWB holsters can even be concealed without an outer garment and with the shirt tucked in. There is a trade off for this level of concealment. Even the best IWB holsters are not quite as comfortable as most outside-the-pants holsters, but with the better IWB designs this comfort difference is negligible. This chapter is a discussion of various belt holsters and the relative advantages and disadvantages of each.

The Belt

A commonly overlooked component of belt holsters is the belt. The importance of a good holster belt for belt carry cannot be stressed enough. Although it is the anchor of the belt holster system, few people give much thought to the belt. A good holster belt will keep the gun firmly in place, even during extreme physical activities such as running or jumping. This is important for two reasons. You want your gun to remain in exactly the same place on your body even during physical activity so that when you reach for your gun to draw, it will be where you expect it to be. If your gun shifts position with your movements, it will cause you to lose precious seconds fumbling to find your grip. The second and most obvious reason for selecting a good belt is that you want to retain the gun on your person. A flimsy belt will not hold the holster in place, and this can cause concealment problems as well as the aforementioned tactical problem of retaining the gun.

The ideal holster belt for concealed carry will provide good vertical and torsional strength without being too wide. This usually means a leather belt, since most fabric belts have poor lateral strength. However, the currently popular braided leather belt makes a poor holster belt since it has virtually no lateral support and is easily twisted. Many holster suppliers offer good belts ranging from 1.25 inches to 1.75 inches in width. The wider the belt, the more conspicuous it looks, particularly with the current trend towards narrower belts. Many of today's trousers have belt loops that will not accommodate a belt wider than 1.5 inches, so check your trousers before you buy a belt (or vice versa.) A 1.5 inch wide belt is the largest width belt that can be used with most popular jeans. A more expensive option is to have a tailor widen your belt loops, but with the many choices of top-quality belts in standard widths this should not be necessary. Other features offered are contoured belts, double layered leather belts, and fiber or poly reinforced belts. Contoured or naturally curved belts will prevent the "kink" that develops in the back of the belt at the middle rear belt loop after the belt has been worn for a period of time. Contoured belts make exceptionally comfortable gun belts. Double layered or poly reinforced belts offer more vertical strength or support in the belt. Until you have worn a good holster belt, you cannot truly appreciate the difference it makes. A good belt makes the belt/holster system remarkably stable. You owe it to yourself to at least try a top-quality belt that was made specifically for supporting the weight of a handgun.

Thumb Breaks

Many belt, shoulder and ankle holsters are offered with the option of a thumb break. A thumb break is a strap that fastens around the gun to keep it securely in the holster while still allowing quick access. Most thumb breaks are secured around the gun with a snap fastener, but some thumb breaks use "hook and loop" or Velcro-type fasteners. In general, the snap fastener thumb breaks are quicker to unfasten as well as quieter than the Velcro thumb breaks. Thumb breaks are different from the traditional holster retaining straps in that the fastener is located on the "strong hand thumb" side of the holster. This allows the thumb break to be unfastened with the strong hand thumb as the hand grips the gun to draw it from the holster, thus the name "thumb break." Thumb breaks are much quicker to draw from than the traditional

A thumb break holster versus an open top holster. The holster on the left is the Galco "Dual Position Phoenix" containing a Browning High Power. The other holster is a Galco "Avenger" with a Springfield Armory 1911-A1.

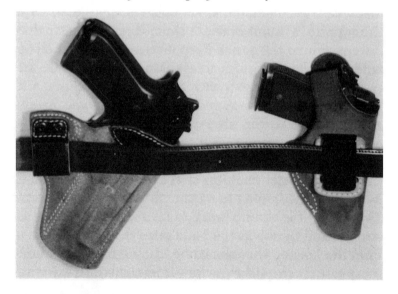

The FBI or forward canted Galco "NSA" holster housing a Beretta 92FS compared to the vertical DeSantis "No. 24" housing a Firestar M40.

holster retaining straps and offer the same security of keeping the gun from accidentally falling out of the holster.

The downside to thumb breaks is that they are slightly slower to draw from than open-top holsters. With practice, this difference can be reduced to tenths of a second. Thumb breaks are fairly controversial; some people swear by them and some people swear at them! Several top quality holster manufacturers will not make holsters with thumb breaks unless expressly requested to do so. These leather artisans believe that a well made, wet molded open-top holster offers a superb fit without the disadvantage of the slightly slower thumb break. Still, many law enforcement agencies require thumb breaks on all belt holsters for their personnel. In the final analysis, thumb breaks are a matter of personal preference, and most popular belt holsters are offered with and without thumb breaks.

Traditional IWB Holsters

Inside-the-waistband holsters (IWBs) are among the most concealable and versatile of all holsters. IWB holsters are actually worn inside the waistband with the grip of the handgun remaining above the belt. Many IWB holsters have a metal or plastic clip that fits over the belt to keep the holster in place. Some of the better IWB holsters have one or more loops that the belt is threaded through to retain the holster. In general, the loops work better than the clips on IWB holsters, but many of the clips work adequately. It is not uncommon to have the clip slip off of the belt and have the entire holster come loose with the gun during a draw. This problem is remedied with the IWB loop holsters. The trade-off is that the IWB clip

Concealed Milt Sparks "Executives Companion" containing a Firestar M40.

Milt Sparks "Executives Companion" with a Firestar M40 under an untucked rugby style shirt.

holsters are typically less expensive than the IWB loop holsters. The IWB clip holsters can also be put on or removed without unbuckling the belt and threading the belt through the holster loop(s). If you use an IWB clip holster, get one with a metal clip. Metal clips have a longer life than plastic clips, and most metal clips grip the belt better than the plastic clips.

IWB holsters are offered with different "cants." The "cant" or "tilt" of a holster is the angle that it rides on the belt. Most inexpensive holsters are not canted; the barrel of the handgun is vertical in the holster when the person wearing the holster is standing. (This is true of virtually all nylon IWB holsters.) Consider a canted holster when shopping for any belt holster. I believe that the forward canted or "FBI cant" has three primary advantages: it blends into the contours of the body better than a vertical holster, it is more comfortable to carry, especially when sitting, and it often offers a better initial grip. Still, different people have different preferences, so use the cant that works best for you.

Some leather IWB holsters are offered with the option of having the leather "rough side out." Although not as aesthetically pleasing as a "smooth side out" holster, a "rough side out" holster is specially suited for in-the-waistband carry. The rough side of the leather has a higher coefficient of friction. This means that once it is put in the waistband, it will be less likely to shift around. This also means that the roughness of the holster will secure the holster in the pants better when the gun is drawn.

The Galco "NSA" with a Beretta 92FS. The NSA can be worn on the left or right side by reversing the belt loop.

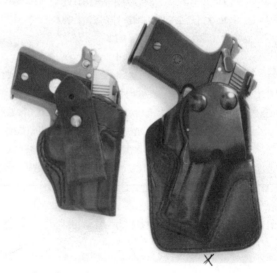

A Kramer "IWB #2" and a Milt Sparks "Executives Companion" designed for a Colt Mustang and a Firestar M40, respectively. These are good examples of molded holsters from custom leather artisans.

One disadvantage of many IWB holsters is that the mouth of the holster collapses after the gun is drawn, making reholstering a two-handed exercise that often cannot be accomplished without looking down to find the holster mouth. Some craftsmen have solved this problem by reinforcing the mouth of the holster with a leather-wrapped metal band. This maintains the comfort of the holster while providing enough rigidity in the holster mouth to keep it open after the gun has been drawn. This feature is especially beneficial to law enforcement personnel who may need to reholster their guns one handed without taking their eyes from a situation.

Another feature some IWB holsters have is a "fairing" around the holster. "Fairing" is extra material or a "flange" around the holster that helps blend the holster's contours to the body versus having a distinct drop off in the lines of the holster. The fairing helps prevent the holster from shifting positions in the pants. The Milt Sparks "Executives Companion" is an example of a "faired" IWB holster. My principal concealed carry choice is one of these "Executives Companion" holsters made for a Firestar M-40 pistol. The "Executives Companion" evolved from the legendary "Summer Special" IWB holster (which was designed by Bruce Nelson of Bruce Nelson Combat Leather and named by Jeff Cooper.) My "Executives Companion" carries the heavy Firestar (30+ ounces unloaded) extremely well. The holster is designed so that it is solidly anchored in the pants and does not shift during normal physical activities. I have worn this rig for 18+ hours at a time during activities ranging from driving and sightseeing to hiking and yard work, and I can whole-heartedly recommend this outstanding holster.

The advantage of IWB holsters is their concealability; the disadvantage is the comfort factor and waist size change. You can wear a well-designed IWB rig all day comfortably, assuming that your pants are 1-2 inches larger in the waist than normal. If you also wear an IWB magazine carrier, you need to experiment to determine which waist size works best. Another disadvantage of the IWB holster is that it exposes your gun to perspiration since it is carried close to the body. Because of this, a gun with a rust/corrosion resistant finish may be preferable to a plain blued finish for IWB carry. In either case, an IWB-carried gun should be inspected and cleaned frequently. (This is also true with any other mode of carry.) Grabbing a handful of shirt when drawing the sidearm is another possibility with IWB holsters.

If you have tried a cheap IWB holster and found it torturous, do not be discouraged. First, make an honest assessment of the handgun you are carrying in the IWB holster. Is it too large for the combination of your body size/type and an IWB holster? Next, look at the holster. Does it have the more comfortable FBI cant? (Most cheap IWB holsters are not canted.) Is the holster designed to distribute the weight of the handgun well? Does the holster have protrusions that uncomfortably dig into your body? Is the holster faired? (Faired holsters tend to distribute the weight of the gun well). Does the holster add excessive bulk to the gun? Are you wearing the holster in the middle of the back (kidney area) or in the more comfortable slightly behind-the-hip configuration? Are your pants too tight even without the holster in the waistband? With the right combination of holster, body type, handgun and clothing, a surprisingly large handgun can be effectively and comfortably concealed in the waistband.

Extremely short barreled handguns and IWB holsters are usually an unhappy marriage. It is simply a matter of geometry; with a short barreled gun, a minimum of the holster extends below the belt in the waistband. This causes the rig to be somewhat top-heavy, and the wearer may feel that the rig is about to slip out of the waistband. In fact, with many IWB holsters for tiny guns, a slight push on the grip of the gun will cause the holster and gun to pop out of the pants. This is not good. Keep such potential problems in mind if you are searching for an IWB holster for a tiny gun. The best bet for an IWB holster for a tiny gun is a faired holster that has more total holster material under and below the belt.

There is a "holsterless" IWB carry method for revolvers that defies easy categorization. The Barami "Hip Grip" is a replacement revolver grip that has a clip built into the grip. The revolver is positioned in the waistband like a traditional IWB holster, and the clip on the grip slips over the belt. In essence, this carries the wheel gun in the waistband like an IWB holster but without actually using a holster. It is fairly comfortable, but it's not as secure during physical activities as a holster. Still, it's a viable low-cost option that fills an important niche.

The majority of IWB holsters are worn on the strong side slightly behind the hip bone with a rearward muzzle rake (FBI cant), but some are worn crossdraw or further back on the strong side in the kidney area. ("Crossdraw" is wearing the gun in front of the weak side hip positioned to be drawn with the strong hand.) One consideration when using an IWB holster is wallet carry. If you are right handed and prefer to wear your gun on your right (strong) side, you will need to wear your wallet in your left rear pocket (versus your right) to prevent the wallet from interfering with the holster. This also reduces the chances of exposing your holster when reaching for your wallet. This sounds trivial, but once you are accustomed to carrying your wallet on one side, it is difficult to get used to wearing it on the other side. This "force of habit" also applies to CCWs in general. Once you are accustomed to a particular type of concealed carry, you may feel uncomfortable without the reassuring weight of your carry gun.

Clothing for Traditional IWB Holsters

Because of their concealability, IWB holsters are ideal for warm weather use. IWB holsters can be effectively concealed with shorts and an untucked shirt, provided that the shirt has a sufficiently long tail. All IWB holsters should be positioned in the pants so that the gun is held close to the body. If there is a gap between the grip of the gun and the body, the concealing garment may unnaturally drape between the holster and body. When using an untucked shirt for concealment, make sure that the holster is not exposed when you bend forward. The "FBI cant" holsters generally conceal the handgun better than vertical holsters, particularly when you are bending. As I have said before, thicker fabrics make better concealing garments for two reasons: the gun cannot be seen through the garment as easily, and the thicker fabrics do not print the gun like thinner fabrics do. This is because thick fabrics are less flexible than thin fabrics thus they do not drape over the gun and outline it like thinner fabrics do. Darker colored clothes conceal better than lighter colors because a wrinkle or bulge is less noticeable on dark fabrics; the bulge easily blends in as a shadow. The rugby shirts that are currently popular are perfect for concealing

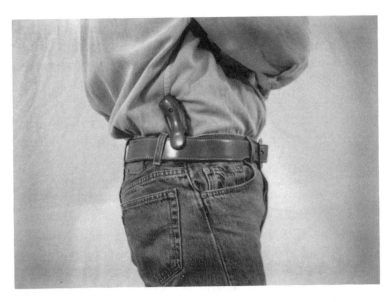

Barami "Hip Grip" on a S&W Chief's Special. Note the Galco "1 1/2 inch Contour" Belt.

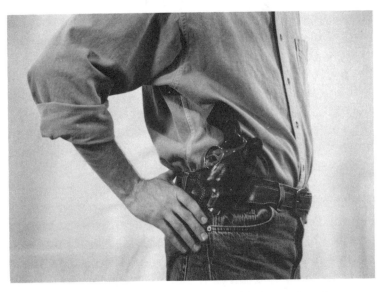

An older model Bianchi "Black Widow" thumb break holster with a Colt Detective Special.

IWB holsters. These shirts are popular for both men and women, they are typically made from heavy weight fabrics, they are in style year-round, and they are fashionable to wear untucked. They are appropriate to wear with shorts, jeans or trousers. Remember, you do not want to be conspicuous, and an untucked rugby shirt is much more common than an untucked Oxford pinpoint button-down.

Several other garments are good for concealing IWB holsters: jackets, sweaters, sweater vests, sweat shirts, warm-up jackets, sports coats, thick shirts and vests. The same rules apply for these clothes as for shirts; look for dark colors, thick fabrics and sufficient length. Some of the longer summer style sweater vests also offer good concealment for IWB holsters. When shopping for a suit coat or sports coat as a concealing garment for a belt holster, look for one that is not "vented." A "vented" coat is one that has one or two 8 -10 inch "slits" that extend up from the rear tail of the coat. Although vented suit coats go in and out of style, they pose two problems as a concealing garment. First, the belt holster may be exposed through the vent when you are bending forward, even though the rest of the coat tail is still covering the holster and gun. Secondly, the vents have a tendency to snag on the handgun and holster, causing the coat to drape unnaturally and expose the holster.

The safari/photojournalist vests like those sold by Banana Republic and Woolrich were mentioned earlier as being a possible hint that the wearer is carrying. In some cities, many off-duty or undercover police officers use these vests for concealed carry. Such vests are great for concealment; they are baggy and have many pockets and flaps that cover any bulges that your handgun may make. They are also much cooler to wear in warm weather than a jacket or other sleeved garment. These vests were designed for travel, so they have numerous handy pockets that police officers (and others) find useful. In most areas of the country they are ideal for concealment, but be aware that many people (especially in urban areas) are savvy to the fact that they are frequently used for concealment. Some of these vests have a see-through interior mesh back covered by a "vented" or split solid back that will not conceal a belt holster well. One remedy for this is to have a seamstress or tailor sew a piece of matching solid material inside the mesh back. This will look like a natural part of the vest but will prevent your holster from being seen through the mesh material. In conclusion, wear clothes that are comfortable and appropriate as well as concealing. You must be confident of two things about your attire: that your clothes conceal your gun well and that they blend into the fashions that are around you.

In his entertaining and informative book *No Second Place Winner*, legendary fast-draw lawman Bill Jordan has a tip for wearers of strong side belt holsters. He advocates carrying some object of slight weight (such as several cartridges) in the strong side coat pocket. This will give the coat some inertia so that once it is swept out of the way during the draw, it will clear the holster and allow the wearer to draw without fumbling with the coat while finding his firing grip. This would also apply to vests worn to conceal a carry gun.

Modified Banana Republic "Photojournalist" safari vest. A Colt Mustang in a K.L. Null "Side Pocket Scabbard" is resting on a piece of material that was added to the interior of the vest. This additional material keeps a belt holster from being seen through the mesh vents on the back of the vest.

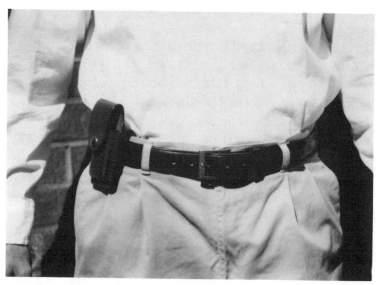

Leatherwood "Hidden Difference" knife sheath holster. Note the Galco "1 1/4 inch Firm System" dress belt.

Below-the-Waistband IWB Holsters

There are several IWB holsters that are not easily categorized. With these holsters the entire gun is concealed beneath the waistband. One is the "Push Up" holster that is made by Galco. The "Push up" is made exclusively for the Seecamp .32 ACP. This holster has a clip that fits over the belt like a traditional IWB holster, but the entire holster is concealed beneath the waistband. The backstrap of the pistol grip is level with the top of the belt. The holster has an open muzzle design, so the barrel protrudes through the end of the holster. To draw the gun, the barrel of the pistol is pushed up from outside of the trousers until the pistol grip is above the waistline. At this point, the pistol can be drawn traditionally. This holster provides a slow draw and accommodates only a low-powered pistol, but it is exceptionally concealable.

Several below the waistband IWB holsters are offered by Leatherwood Holsters. These faired holsters are designed with the gun positioned below the waistband. A knife sheath, like those used for folding lock-blade knives, is mounted onto the holster. The knife sheath slips over the belt and keeps the holster from sliding further beneath the waistband. The same holster is offered with the option of a "dummy" pager/beeper or a pager/beeper case. The manufacturer claims a two to three second draw, with practice, using this holster. While this is not the most accessible holster, it can carry a medium sized semi-automatic with the shirt tucked in and no concealing outer garment. These holsters are slow to draw from, and require you to be standing in order to draw the gun. Since these holsters suspend the gun below the beltline, they do not take advantage of natural body contours. Even a small handgun produces an abnormal bulge on the hip or thigh. Because of comfort, accessibility and concealment, this style of holster is not recommended.

Outside-the-Pants Holsters

Four primary types of outside-the-pants holsters are made especially for concealment: pancake/scabbard holsters, belt slides, paddle holsters, and small of the back holsters. While these holsters take a little more effort to conceal than the IWB holsters, they are usually more comfortable for extended wear. Outside-the-pants holsters typically require an outer garment such as a sweater, jacket or vest for concealment, so they are not quite as versatile as IWB holsters. Because some part of all outside-the-pants holsters extends below the belt, they require a longer concealing garment than the IWB holsters.

Pancake/Scabbard Holsters

Pancake holsters got their name from their thin, low profile design; thus the "flat as a pancake" holster. Pancake and scabbard holsters are virtually identical in design. Pancake holsters typically have the belt slots on either side of the holster to allow the holster to be drawn in close to the body, while scabbard holsters may have only one belt slot. Pancake and scabbard holsters are offered with a variety of options: thumb breaks, open tops, various cants, and open or covered muzzle designs. Many pancake and scabbard holsters are of the "high ride" design. This feature has the gun positioned high on the side and generally with an FBI cant. Such positioning allows the gun and holster to be concealed by a shorter outer garment, but it makes the rig somewhat top-heavy. Some of the better holsters have a tension screw adjust-

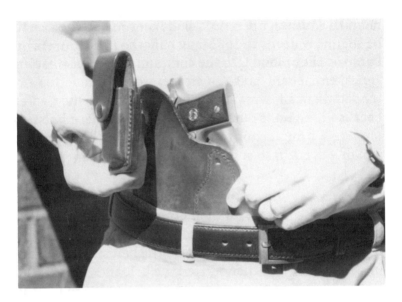

This Leatherwood holster contains a Colt Mustang.

Leatherwood "Hidden Difference" knife sheath holster.

ment that allows the "grip" the holster has on the gun to be set to the user's taste. Many pancake holsters are also faired so they blend into the contours of the body better. Pancake/scabbard holsters are very comfortable for extended wear, allowing a full range of motion to the wearer because the gun is outside of the pants. These holsters provide a firm anchor for your handgun, a combat grip, and one of the fastest draws of any concealment holster.

Belt Slides

Belt slides are famous for their economy of material. Most belt slides are just that: a slide or loop that the belt is threaded through. Depending on the belt slide used, the handgun is worn either outside the belt and through the slide or between the belt and trousers and through the slide. The advantages of a belt slide are its lack of excess materials and the fact that without a handgun in it, many belt slides are not easily identified as holsters. This may be desirable for people who want to wear their holster all the time in case the need arises to actually carry their gun. In this case, they already have their holster on their belt and no one is the wiser. The disadvantages of belt slides include lack of security and the propensity of the front sights of the gun to snag on the belt slide since the barrel is "unguided" during the first few inches of the draw. (By the time the front sights are about to be drawn through the belt slide, they can hang up on the bottom of the belt slide.) With the cheaper belt slides the slide is not fitted properly to the gun, which can lead to the gun coming out of the holster at an inappropriate time. One of the best belt slides available is the "Belt Slide Holster" made by Mitchell Rosen of Mitchell's Leatherworks. This holster is molded to the particular model gun that it is to be used with for a secure fit. This slide also has a molded sight track to prevent the sight from snagging on the slide.

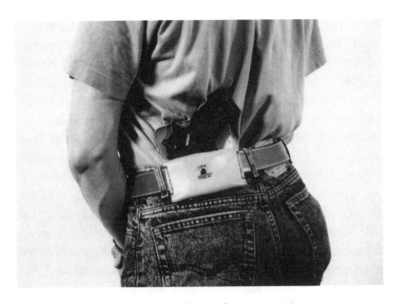

LAW Concealment "LCS II" IWB holster with a Beretta 92FS.

"Old West" belt slide with a Browning High Power.

Paddle Holsters

Paddle holsters have a thin paddle-shaped piece of material attached to a traditional looking outside-the-pants holster. The "paddle," which may be constructed of leather, plastic or some other combination of materials, is inserted into the waistband. The paddle material is usually flexible so that it conforms to the shape of the user's hip. This paddle keeps the holster securely positioned so that it will not shift. Some of the paddle holsters also have a loop that the belt can be threaded through to keep the holster from coming out of the pants with the gun during a draw. Paddle holsters are offered with different cants and carrying heights. Paddle holsters have three primary advantages: they can be donned and removed easily, they are more comfortable than an IWB rig since only a thin paddle is in the pants versus the entire gun, and they do not require a belt. The paddle holster can be removed without taking off the belt, and this option is attractive to many. Paddle holsters are also a good solution because they can be used with beltless slacks (or a skirt) or for individuals who do not like to wear belts. The disadvantage of the paddle holster is that it, too, is more difficult to conceal than the IWB holster.

Small-of-the-Back Holster (SOB)

This rig has gained some notoriety simply from its acronym. The name of this holster is fairly self-explanatory; it rides in a horizontal position on the belt in the middle of the back. These SOB holsters are popular among people who do a lot of standing (versus reclining against chairs or vehicle seats.) SOB holsters are very handy to use while riding motorcycles, ATVs, bicycles or horses because these

Safariland "Hi Ride Paddle" holster with a Beretta 92FS.

Safariland "Hi Ride Paddle" holster - Note the tension adjustment screw.

activities do not require you to recline against anything. SOB holsters do not get in the way as much as other outside-the-pants holsters when bending at the waist is involved. Also, they do not require as long an outer garment for concealment as the other outside-the-pants holsters.

On the down-side, the SOB holsters are not as comfortable when you are reclining as the other outside-the-pants holsters are. Also, at least one major holster maker will not make an SOB holster because of the risk of serious injury if you fall on your back while wearing the SOB holster and gun. Carrying any hard object at the base of the spine puts you at risk of a spinal cord injury, and police officers have reportedly been paralyzed after falling on their handcuffs that were carried in the small of the back. Another disadvantage of SOB holsters arises when driving a car. The SOB holster is the most difficult of the above-the-waistband belt holsters to access when sitting in a car. With today's threat of carjacking, this is a serious limitation.

Clothing choices for outside-the-pants holsters are similar to that of IWB holsters with these exceptions: an untucked shirt alone is usually inadequate to conceal an outside-the-pants belt holster, and any concealing outer garment needs to be slightly longer to conceal an outside-the-pants holster.

Paddle-side view of the Safariland "Hi Ride Paddle" holster.

Crossdraw Belt Holsters

Many of the above mentioned holsters may be worn in a crossdraw fashion. The advantages of crossdraw are speed and access. A gun worn crossdraw can be readily reached while seated, and this is particularly an advantage in a car. Crossdraw wear also allows the quickest and easiest access of any belt holster with the weak hand in the event the strong hand is immobile or disabled. When carrying a handgun crossdraw with a jacket or vest for concealment, you can simply reach into the garment through the front to access the weapon. When carrying strong side, the outer garment must be swept out of the way to reach the gun, and this is slightly slower. Crossdraw carry has two major disadvantages: the gun is positioned so that it can be easily grabbed by an assailant who may be facing you, and crossdraw wear nearly always requires an outer garment for concealment. Because the shape of the body forward of the hip prevents the gun from being pulled in close against the body, an untucked shirt often will not adequately conceal even an IWB crossdraw holster. If a suit coat is worn to conceal a crossdraw holster, it must remain buttoned for effective concealment. However, because of the position of the holster, the gun can often be drawn by reaching in without having to unbutton the coat. Another school of thought focuses on the speed of the crossdraw; many believe that it is faster on the draw than the other types of belt holsters. Like all of the other holster options, it boils down to personal preference. If you prefer crossdraw carry, then that is what you will practice, and you will subsequently become faster using the crossdraw carry. One final caution about crossdraw carry; unless the draw is executed perfectly, the muzzle of the gun will cross some part of the wearer's body, which presents a safety hazard under stress.

Conclusion - Which Belt Holster to Use?

Choosing a belt holster involves many factors: body shape, handgun model, weather, normal daily activities and normal wardrobe. The IWB and below-the-waistband holsters are more concealable, but the outside-the-pants holsters are more comfortable. From the fastest to slowest in accessibility, the outside-the-pants holsters are the fastest, with the IWB holsters slightly behind in speed, and the below-the-waistband holsters a distant third. Finally, the choice is a personal one that must take your lifestyle into account. There is no "right" answer except this: choose a holster with which you can confidently and comfortably conceal your handgun on a daily basis. If you do not wear the gun, you will not have it around when you most need it.

One final word of caution about all belt holsters; be aware of the types of chairs in which you sit when wearing a belt holster. If you wear your holster rear of your hipbone and sit in a chair that does not have a solid back (as in many restaurants,) you run the risk of having your gun "catch" on the chair as you sit down, stand up or turn. This should not prevent you from sitting in this type of chair, but you should be aware of this potential problem. For example, if given a choice in a restaurant, sitting in a padded booth or chair is preferable to a slot-backed chair when you are wearing a belt holster.

Chapter 3
SHOULDER, ANKLE, AND POCKET HOLSTERS

In the category of traditional holsters, shoulder and ankle holsters are a distant second and third behind belt holsters in terms of popularity. Indeed, the overexposure of shoulder holsters on TV and in movies suggests that they are more popular than they really are. There are two reasons for this disparity: shoulder holsters are more exotic than belt holsters, and shoulder holsters photograph better than belt holsters. You wouldn't expect James Bond to tool around Monte Carlo in a "plain Jane" belt holster would you? That's not to say that shoulder, ankle, and pocket holsters do not have their place; they most certainly do.

Shoulder Holsters

There are many versions of shoulder holsters, and all are suspended by at least one strap that passes over one or both shoulders for support. Many shoulder holster harnesses are designed in a figure eight in which each arm is inserted into one of the loops of the figure eight with the center of the harness resting on the top part of the back and shoulders. The gun is carried under the weak arm so that it can be drawn with the strong hand. A variety of accessories may be carried attached to the harness under

DeSantis "Slant Shoulder Rig" with Firestar M40.

Rear view of the DeSantis "Slant Shoulder Rig."

the strong hand, ranging from spare magazines or speed loaders to handcuff cases. The harness may also be further secured via a "tie down," which is a strap that secures the holster harness to the belt. The gun may be carried horizontally, vertically or canted, depending upon the style of holster. Most holsters can be adjusted to fit a variety of body sizes, and most horizontal holsters can be adjusted until the cant of the gun is to your liking. The most concealable and the fastest drawing shoulder holsters carry the gun nearly vertical with a slight muzzle-up cant. This allows the gun to be drawn smoothly and in a natural fashion. Thumb breaks are often used to secure the gun in the holster, but some models rely on a holster tensioning screw to retain the handgun.

Shoulder holsters have several advantages. A well-designed and fitted shoulder holster can be comfortable, even for extended wear. The shoulder rigs with the better harnesses do a good job of distributing the weight of the gun and accessories over the shoulders, versus having the weight concentrated in one area. Including the gun, most shoulder rigs do not weigh any more than a heavy winter coat, and they can be just as comfortable as a coat. Shoulder rigs also allow for the comfortable carry of spare magazines and other accessories. A shoulder holster can be weight balanced easier than many holsters when a double magazine case is worn under the strong arm as an accessory. One tactical advantage of a shoulder holster is the ability to draw while seated. This makes a shoulder holster useful in a car, but be aware that the design of some automobile safety belts necessitates that you practice drawing from your shoulder holster while buckled up. Shoulder holsters can also be a wise choice for cold weather carry. The handgun in a shoulder rig can be nonchalantly reached through a long overcoat even if the

Holster-side - Note the thumb break.

Off-side - Note the dual magazine pouch that helps weight balance this rig.

coat is still partially zipped or buttoned up.   A long overcoat that is unfastened down to the mid-chest level will still provide ready access to the carry gun; this is not the case with a belt holster since the coat must be "swept away" to access the gun in a belt holster.   It is important that the outer garment you use with a shoulder holster is not too restrictive.   You will need to be able to reach across your body to grip your gun without being hindered by a too-tight concealing garment.

Shoulder holsters have some disadvantages, though. Shoulder holsters require a sleeved outer garment for concealment.   This eliminates vests as concealment wear, because the shoulder holster harness can be seen through the arm opening of a vest.   Even if you are wearing a coat, shoulder holsters are often visible when bending forward, since the concealing outer garment has a tendency to open when you lean forward.   This necessitates either being aware of your actions and not letting your coat open when you bend forward or keeping your coat buttoned. As is the case with a crossdraw holster, because it is carried butt-forward, a gun in a shoulder rig is vulnerable to being snatched by an attacker.   Shoulder holsters are typically hard to conceal on a thin person, and the harness material that is used in a shoulder holster must be concealed as well as the holster.   Also, shoulder holster adjustments are difficult to do alone, and a well adjusted shoulder rig will substantially improve comfort and concealability.   If not adjusted properly, the "X" in the harness will flex and be visible through your concealing garment during some movements (like bending.) Another consideration is that, on the average, a quality shoulder holster is significantly more expensive that a belt holster of the same quality, simply because the shoulder holster requires more material.

Galco "Ankle Holster" for a Beretta 950 BBS. Note that the holster is tucked into the sock for better concealment if the trouser leg rides up.

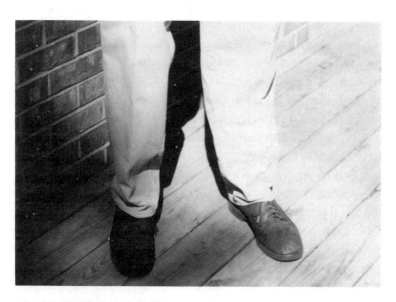

Galco "Ankle Holster" concealed..

Finally, shoulder holster carry, like crossdraw carry, requires you to cover some part of your body with the muzzle during the draw or reholstering of your gun. A classic case is holding the shoulder holster with the weak hand while drawing; this has resulted in more than one wounded weak hand. Some long-time shoulder holster wearers believe that semi-auto safeties are likely to snag on a shoulder holster, so they favor revolvers for shoulder holster carry.

Ankle Holsters

There are two basic kinds of below-the-knee leg holsters: those that are carried around the upper portion of the calf and those that are worn around the ankle. The calf holster is not as apt to be exposed if you cross your legs when seated, but the ankle holster offers appreciably faster access. Most ankle holsters are worn on the inside of the weak leg so they can be more easily reached with the strong hand, and when worn in this position they are not as susceptible to being "bumped" into something. They may be made of leather, ballistic nylon or an elasticized fabric. Many ankle rigs are made with a padded backing for a more comfortable fit. As with any holster, some people fall in love with their ankle holsters while others may never grow accustomed to the extra weight on one leg. One way to improve ankle holster concealment is to tuck the lower portion of the holster into your sock. This way, even if the cuff of the pants slides up, the holster will not be apparent since it is covered by the sock.

Ankle holsters have the advantage of being easily accessible while the wearer is seated. For this reason the wearer may use them effectively while driving. Also, ankle rigs can be reached when the wearer is lying flat on his back. More than one policeman has saved his life and the lives of others by being able to reach his ankle gun while an assailant was wrestling with him. In this situation, a belt or shoulder holster may not be easily reached if your body weight and/or the weight of an attacker is on top of the gun. An ankle rig can also be reached with the strong or weak hand, in the event that one hand is disabled. Ankle holsters can be effectively concealed with only a short sleeved shirt and trousers; neither an outer garment or untucked shirt is required.

On the downside, ankle holsters are generally slow to draw from. It is difficult to casually reach your gun in an ankle rig while you are standing. While you can nonchalantly grip your handgun when it is in a shoulder or belt holster without drawing undue attention to your actions, to do so with an ankle holster is unnatural. The exception is if you are able to rest your leg on an object such as a car bumper with the pretense of tying your shoe. Ankle rigs require long pants, so they are often not appropriate for extremely hot weather. Unless bell-bottomed jeans come back into style, ankle rigs can not be worn with jeans because of the narrow legs of the styles popular today. Even with flared trouser legs, a full-sized handgun can not be carried in an ankle holster effectively, so you are limited to medium-sized guns and smaller guns for ankle carry. Because of this size limitation, ankle rigs are best used for a back-up gun. The poor weight distribution of ankle holsters is another factor to consider. Ankle holsters are the most difficult holsters to weight balance because the weight is in the position of the greatest leverage: at the end of the leg.

Ankle rigs also have the disadvantage of being close to the ground; for this reason the ankle-carried gun picks up more dirt, grime, water, and snow than guns concealed in other ways. These hazards are all potential reliability nightmares; dirt and grime may cause the gun to malfunction, snow and water may refreeze in cold weather to render the handgun useless. These hazards must be taken into account, and the ankle-carried gun must be inspected before and after each time it is carried and subsequently cleaned as necessary. Because of this, a revolver typically makes a better ankle gun than a pistol. Revolvers are more forgiving of infrequent maintenance, but any handgun carried in this fashion should be examined each time the holster is strapped on.

In summary, ankle holsters are better used for back-up holsters rather than primary holsters, but an ankle rig is infinitely better than no gun at all.

Pocket Holsters

Pocket holsters can be divided into three basic categories: front pants pocket holsters, rear pants pocket or wallet holsters, and coat or vest pocket holsters. Many small guns can be inconspicuously carried in pockets, so this convenient option should not be overlooked. In some states it is illegal to carry a gun in a pocket without a holster even if you have a concealed carry permit. There are other good reasons not to carry a gun loose in a pocket: the gun will not be properly positioned for drawing, the gun may print through the pocket, and the gun may get dirty from being carried loose in the pocket.

There are several variations of the simple scabbard style pocket holster. These holsters will keep the gun relatively clean as well as breaking up the outline of the gun. They

The right front pocket contains a Colt Mustang in a Kramer "Pocket Holster", while a Beretta 950 BBS is in a DeSantis "Trickster" holster in the left front pocket.

Note that the Kramer holster is designed to be carried in the right pocket. This holster has a piece of plastic laminate sewn onto the side of the holster that faces away from the body. This helps break up the outline of the holster in the pocket, and causes the bulge in the pocket to look like a wallet.

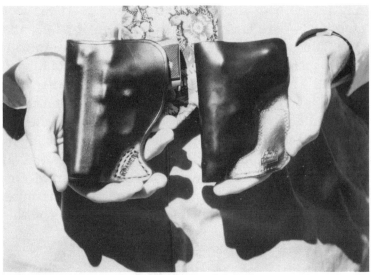

Rear view of the Kramer "Pocket Holster" and the DeSantis "Trickster."

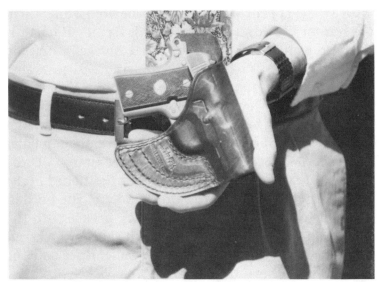

The Ken L. Null "Side Pocket Scabbard" holster designed for a Colt Mustang Nite Lite. This holster works especially well in a coat or vest pocket.

may be worn in the front or rear pocket. One good example is "The Trickster," which is made by DeSantis. "The Trickster" is made for very small semi-automatic pistols such as the Seecamp .32 and the Beretta Models 950 and 21. Galco and Kramer Handgun Leather both make a version of the scabbard style pocket holster that is designed not to shift in the pocket. This keeps the gun positioned so that it can be reached without fumbling for it. These holsters are also designed to snag and stay in the pocket when the gun is drawn, a worthwhile feature. One trick to reduce the printing of a gun through a front trouser pocket is to have a tailor line the carry pocket with a chamois or canvas type material.

Another version of the pocket holster is the wallet holster. These are made both for derringers and small semi-autos. The theory is that if a mugger asks for your wallet, you can "Let him have it!" Some wallet holsters are made with a trigger opening so the gun can be fired while still in the holster. However, be forewarned: a semi-automatic is likely to malfunction from the ejected brass hitting the wallet. When using a semi-automatic with a wallet holster it is best to remove the pistol from the holster before firing. However, some wallet holsters are designed with an opening for ejected brass. There are now wallet holsters made for small/medium sized semi-automatics like the AMT Back-Up and the Colt Mustang. These holsters are designed so that the gun is positioned in the holster with the muzzle toward the fold of the holster. The holster is then worn in the back pocket with the muzzle up. With this design, even if the holster sticks out of the pocket it will look like a large wallet since only the leather "wallet" is protruding from the pocket. To draw the gun using this holster, you must retrieve the holster out of the pocket and then pull the gun from the holster to achieve a firing grip, since the grip of the gun is carried at the bottom of the pocket.

One consideration when carrying a wallet holster is your actual wallet. You do not want to have a "two wallet" look. Strong Holster Company has solved this dilemma by offering their ultra-thin front pocket wallet. This wallet has space for money and ID, but little else. It can easily be carried in a front pants pocket or coat pocket and will prevent the strange image of carrying two wallets.

A pocket holster designed for revolvers is Pachmayr's "Tactical Pocket Holster." This polymer holster clips onto a J-frame S&W revolver. The holster is designed to remain attached to the gun when the gun is fired. The holster has a hammer shroud that keeps the hammer from snagging in the pocket but still allows the revolver to be fired single action, if so desired. The "Tactical Pocket Holster" also can carry five spare rounds of ammo, and the entire holster effectively breaks up the outline of the revolver in the pocket. Due to the size of this holster/gun combination, it is best used in a large coat pocket.

LAW Concealment offers a pouch type "in the waistband" holster that may also be used in an interior coat pocket. This LAW holster can clip into the pocket and keep the handgun secured and properly positioned. With a heavy coat, even a large handgun can be effectively concealed. The disadvantage of carrying any holster in a coat pocket is that once you take off your coat, you may not be positioned to access the gun as easily as when you are still wearing the coat. Weight balancing is a must for a heavy gun that is carried in a coat pocket. Unless a similarly

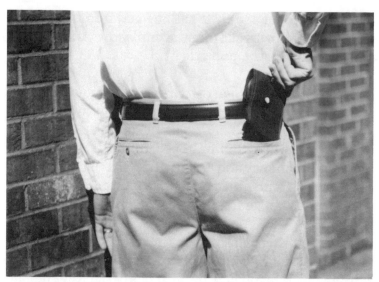

A generic ballistic nylon wallet holster for the High Standard derringer. Note the trigger access hole in the holster that allows the derringer to be fired while still in the holster.

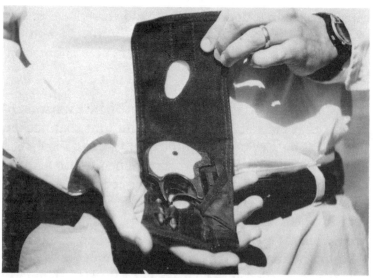

Opened wallet holster - Note the loops for carrying two extra cartridges.

weighted object is carried in the opposite pocket, the coat will hang oddly off your frame. This is especially notice-able on a windy day; one side of the coat will remain in place, while the other sways in the breeze.

The chief advantage of pocket holsters is often over-looked: convenience. Good pocket holsters are one of the best kept secrets of western civilization. They do not get much attention because they lack the nostalgic appeal of belt, ankle and shoulder holsters. (Neither Bogie, Cagney or Eastwood would be caught dead with a pocket holster!) However, nearly all trousers conveniently have front and rear pockets that are capable of carrying small handguns. It is easy to conceal a tiny semi-auto like a Beretta Model 950 or a Seecamp .32 in the front pocket of a pair of Duck Head-style shorts wearing only the shorts and a tucked-in tee shirt. With the advent of super small, medium powered, lightweight pistols like the Colt Mustang Pocket Lite in .380 caliber, a respectably powered pistol can be carried in a pocket. If the clothing must be minimal, a pocket holster is tough to beat. Comfort is also an advantage of pocket holsters; with many small handguns a good pocket holster is so comfortable that it is possible to forget that you are armed. Another advantage is cost; since pocket holsters merely position the gun and keep it free from debris versus actually bearing the load of the gun, they are generally less expensive than the other traditional options. There is also a significant tactical advantage using a front or wallet pocket holster in that it is easy for the wearer to casually access the gun without looking conspicuous. Nonchalantly putting your hand in your front pants pocket or reaching for your wallet is a common gesture. This allows you to achieve a firing grip without ever exposing your gun.

A collection of pocket holsters shown with a deck of playing cards for size comparison. From the top; Kramer "Pocket Holster" for a Colt Mustang, generic wallet holster for a High Standard derringer, DeSantis "Trickster" holster for a Beretta 950 BBS, Pachmayr "Tactical Pocket Holster" with a S&W Chief's Special, and the K.L. Null "Side Pocket Scabbard" for a Colt Mustang.

The biggest drawback to pocket holsters is the size of the gun that can be carried in a pocket. It is not practical to carry a government model .45 in ANY trouser pocket, but this same gun may be carried in a coat pocket. Another advantage of a coat pocket is the ability to crudely point and fire a handgun through a coat pocket in an emergency. Pocket holsters do not afford the fastest draw of any holster, but obtaining a firing grip before telegraphing your intentions makes up for much of this lack of speed.

The bottom line is that pocket holsters are convenient and comfortable, but a large handgun cannot be effectively concealed in a pocket (with the possible exception of an overcoat pocket.) Still, during a lethal confrontation the tiny .380 you have in your pocket is much more useful than the full sized .45 you left at home.

Chapter 4
ACCESSORY HOLSTERS

Regardless of the clothes that you wear, there is an accessory holster that can enable you to conceal a handgun under virtually any circumstances. The proliferation of many well-thought-out accessory holster designs greatly increases your options for concealed carry. One of the most common accessory holsters is the ubiquitous fanny pack.

Fanny Packs

Fanny packs were originally designed for day hikers. The premise was that for short recreational hikes, a full sized back pack was not needed. The fanny pack got its name because the original fanny packs were worn fastened around the waist with the pack in the back. These packs were small, lightweight, and easily put on or removed, yet they still provided a means for carrying small items while keeping the hands free for other tasks. Fanny packs grew in popularity, and eventually skiers, rock climbers, cyclists and tourists were regularly using these handy packs. As they became commonplace, the evolution of fanny packs as concealment holsters was a natural.

Customized Bianchi "KO Fanny Pack".

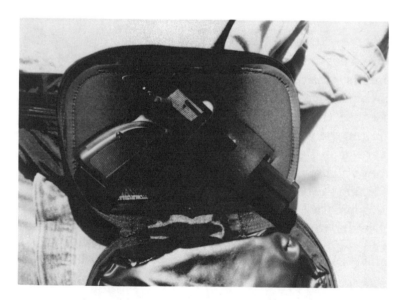

Opened fanny pack revealing a Browning High Power.

The first fanny pack holsters offered people of all body types an opportunity to carry a full-sized handgun with virtually no clothing restrictions. No longer was a sports coat required for concealed carry; now a large handgun could be carried while wearing only shorts and a tee shirt. The DeSantis "Gunny Sack" is generally credited as the first of this new breed. This first generation of fanny pack holsters was very successful with both undercover police officers and people who wanted to carry a concealed handgun when participating in outdoor recreational activities. These first fanny pack holsters did not have more widespread use because it was still not fashionable for men to wear fanny packs. However, over the last several years the popularity of fanny packs for general use has skyrocketed among both sexes. Because of this popularity and acceptance for use with both sexes, fanny packs are less conspicuous than ever.

Most holster fanny packs are designed to be worn with the pack in front of the hip, so the name is something of a misnomer. For a right handed person, the pack is generally worn in front of the left hip. This allows you to open the pack with your weak hand and draw the gun with your strong hand. Most packs are made of ballistic nylon, but models are also available in leather. The typical fanny pack has a strap that fastens around the waist with a simple three pronged clip. These straps can be clipped on quickly, but they can also be unclipped easily and snatched by an experienced thief. The front opening of most packs is secured either with a Velcro-type fastener or a dual zipper arrangement. Most zipper packs can be opened quickly with a ripcord that sticks out of the zippers and allows the front of the pack to be snatched open. Many packs have a separate compartment for the handgun and another main compartment for other items. Some packs also have other small compartments on either side of the holster compartment for miscellaneous items. Fanny pack holsters come in a variety of sizes to fit most handguns. The holster compartment of most packs is backed with a semi-rigid material that provides a firm foundation for the handgun. This backing, usually plastic, keeps the pack from sagging and helps keep the handgun positioned properly. The actual holster in the pack is usually a loop or a slot in an elastic material, often with a Velcro strap that can be fastened over the grip of the handgun like a thumb break for a more secure carry. As you are choosing a fanny pack, one consideration is whether to go with a Velcro fastened front opening or a zipper arrangement. When opened quickly, both of these types make a distinctive noise. However, the zipper closure can be opened quietly when unzipped slowly. It is virtually impossible to open the Velcro closure quietly, but this type of fanny pack has a slight speed of access advantage over a zipper fanny pack. Also, the packs with the zipper closures require finer motor skills, and a zipper can fail and stick in place, causing an access problem. When selecting a fanny pack holster, the choice between a zipper or Velcro closure is too close to call (as is evidenced by both models' popularity.)

Fanny pack holsters have several advantages. A large handgun and spare magazine or speed loader can be concealed effectively by anyone, regardless of body type. Fanny packs do not require a concealing outer garment; thus, they can be worn in warm weather without excessive clothing. Fanny packs can be strapped on or removed easily and quickly, and they blend in when worn in tourist areas or during outdoor athletic activities. Fanny packs can also be used with different guns since most packs can accommodate a variety of gun sizes. Because the gun is carried forward of the hip with fanny pack holsters, they are good for driving or other seated activities. The excellent weight distribution of most fanny packs provides comfort during extended carry.

Fanny pack holsters also have disadvantages. A fanny pack can be stolen fairly easily either by unfastening the strap buckle or by cutting the strap. Also, fanny packs cannot be used as a single all-purpose concealed carry holster because they are not socially appropriate for all occasions. Fanny packs are not especially good for cold weather carry, since a coat or jacket worn over the fanny pack will make drawing from the fanny pack difficult.

Because of the popularity of fanny pack holsters, they are no longer a secret. If you have a working knowledge of the various types of fanny pack holsters, it is not difficult to spot fanny packs that are actually holsters. First, look for black fanny packs since this is the most popular color for fanny pack holsters. Secondly, because of the semi-rigid backing material in most fanny pack holsters, they do not sag like the cheaper non-holster fanny packs. Another hint that a fanny pack may be concealing a gun is the ripcord that is used on many of the zipper style packs. This ripcord conspicuously protrudes from the pack. One remedy is to either remove the ripcord or leave it inside the pack while leaving a small gap between the zippers unzipped. This allows the thumb of the weak hand to reach into the pack to yank the pack open versus pulling the ripcord. In my experience, this is both more discreet and more reliable; I believe that it is easier to quickly open the pack by using this "zipper gap" than by using the ripcord. The absence of zippers on a Velcro-closed fanny pack also may indicate that it is a holster pack, since most generic fanny packs use zippers instead of Velcro to secure the front opening of the pack.

There are several ways to customize a fanny pack holster to make it look like it is not a holster pack. For starters, many of the fanny pack holster suppliers now offer their packs in a variety of colors other than black, from navy blue to hot pink to neon yellow. These non-black fanny packs look less like holster packs, and the wilder the color the better. Another good idea is to add a patch or some other insignia to the fanny pack. One option would be to sew a patch with the name or mascot of a local college or university onto the pack. This would also work with any type of patch, ranging from "The Mickey Mouse Fan Club" to "Eat more possum." However, a patch that states "NRA Life Member," "Insured by Smith & Wesson," or "Kill 'em all and let God sort 'em out" lacks the subtlety needed to disguise the holster fanny pack. Still another idea would be to embroider your name or initials onto the fanny pack. Since fanny packs are also given away as promotional items by many companies, sewing a corporate name or logo onto a holster fanny pack is another way to disguise it. If the holster fanny pack has the name of the manufacturer or a brand name on it, remove this if possible. This would be a dead giveaway to anyone familiar with that brand.

The bottom line is that fanny pack holsters are very versatile, expanding your concealed carry options. They are comfortable and especially convenient for moderately active recreational activities. On the downside, fanny pack holsters are very popular, thus many people are wise to them. Minor effort put towards customizing a fanny pack will pay large dividends in better concealment.

Camera/Belt Case Holsters

Similar to fanny pack holsters, camera case or belt case holsters offer additional versatility. A camera case holster is simply a case that resembles a belt camera case that either clips onto the belt, has belt loops, or both. These cases come in different sizes to accommodate handguns from a tiny .25 to a full-sized Government Model .45. These belt case holsters have the opening of the case fastened either with a Velcro fastener or a dual zipper arrangement, similar to a fanny pack holster.

Camera case holsters have the advantage of looking like innocent belt camera cases. By the same token, since they look like camera cases, they are limited in their applications. If the situation is not appropriate for a camera, then a camera case holster would be conspicuous. These holsters are perfect for tourist areas or other events where cameras are widely used. A danger is that cameras are often the target of muggers, so a camera case holster may draw undesirable attention. This makes a belt case holster that has belt loops in addition to a belt clip desirable, since the case cannot be snatched as easily if the belt is threaded through the case. In some areas belt cases, like fanny packs, are gaining in popularity with both men and women as a convenient means to carry small items "hands free." In these areas, camera case holsters can be used without causing suspicion.

One worthwhile modification to a belt/camera case holster is the addition of a name-brand camera label to the case. Simply take a label off of an actual camera case and sew it onto the camera case holster. This is especially useful for the larger holster cases that are bigger than most camera cases. A cheaper name brand label will draw less attention from potential camera snatchers than a "Nikon" label.

Customized Bagmaster "Belt Pistol Pack" holster.

Opened belt/camera case to reveal a Firestar M40.

As small cellular phones become more popular, it is likely that many people will use belt cases for their phones, making belt case holsters even less conspicuous for everyday use.

Portfolio Holsters

Portfolio holsters look like conventional over-the-shoulder carry bags. They can be made from a variety of materials, including ballistic nylon, leather and canvas. Most portfolio holsters have a separate compartment for the handgun. This holster compartment is closed either with a zipper or a Velcro strip that looks like a seam in the material. The Velcro seam is slightly faster to access, but the zipper is less likely to come open accidentally. Many portfolio holsters also have another compartment that can accommodate a panel of Kevlar body armor. Some of the portfolios that have the body armor compartment have a strap that can be placed around the head so the portfolio can actually be worn as makeshift body armor after the handgun has been withdrawn from the portfolio holster. Many portfolios also have steel bands enclosed in the shoulder strap. These steel bands are designed to keep the shoulder strap from being easily cut by the knife or scissors of a snatch-and-run thief.

While concealment portfolios are offered in a variety of styles to suit most tastes, do not overlook the advantages of creating your own. You can start with a popular name-brand bag that will never be suspected of concealing a gun. You can have it built to your exact tastes (including a Kevlar panel, if so desired), and you may even save some money. Any competent seamstress or tailor should be able to modify a fabric portfolio to your specifications, and probably a leather one as well. You can have the holster of your choice sewn in, or make a custom holster of elastic and Velcro. When completed, you'll have a unique bag that meets your requirements and that no one will suspect.

The portfolio holster has the advantage of being appropriate for men and women. A portfolio holster can also accommodate nearly any sized handgun, as well as spare magazines or speed loaders. A portfolio holster is ideal for people who need a handgun primarily for the walk from a car, bus, or subway to their place of work. Also, a portfolio holster might be appropriate for college students who have a dangerous walk from car to dwelling. However, many states have laws prohibiting guns near schools, so use near campus may not be legal. Over-the-shoulder portfolios are widely used by the general public, so a holster portfolio offers excellent concealment.

As for negatives, a portfolio would be out of place at a movie theater or a shopping mall. Portfolio holsters fill a specific niche, so they are not a good choice for an all-purpose holster. Since the handgun is carried in the portfolio and not actually on your body, there exists a tactical problem because your handgun is only as close as your portfolio. If you put your portfolio down and leave it, you are defenseless.

Day-Planner Holsters

One of the latest entries on the concealed accessory holster scene is the day-planner holster. This holster looks like a generic 8.5" by 11" zip-up day-planner notebook. When the notebook is opened, it unfolds to reveal a holster.

This holster has most of the same advantages and disadvantages of the portfolio holster while being even more portable. Many professional men and women keep their day-planners with them all day, so this holster would not be out of place in most urban areas during business hours. A day-planner holster will accommodate a 1911 .45, so this is one way for people of all body types to conceal a full-size handgun effectively.   One drawback of the day-planner holster not shared by the portfolio holster is that it requires at least one hand for carrying the day-planner at all times.   The day-planner is more apt to be laid down to free the hands for some other task.   This makes the handgun in the day-planner holster more likely to fall into the wrong hands.

Chapter 5
MISCELLANEOUS CONCEALED CARRY HOLSTERS

T his chapter covers some of the many miscellaneous concealed carry holsters that do not fit into any of the traditional holster categories. This chapter does not attempt to cover every other possible holster, just those that are practical and commercially available. With a little effort and ingenuity, the possibilities for other concealed carry holsters are limitless.

"Belly Band" Holsters

There are several different types of under-the-shirt/coat elastic band or "Belly Band" holsters. Most types are constructed of elastic bands that wrap around the waist or chest and are fastened with Velcro-type patches. A pocket that holds the handgun is sewn in the band, and several manufacturers offer a Velcro-type thumb break to secure the gun in the elastic band pocket. Many models that fit around the chest also have straps on the handgun side of the band that fit over the shoulder like suspenders. Such shoulder straps help bear the weight of the handgun to prevent the band from sagging and sliding down the torso under load. Belly band holsters are sized, and they are sold by the standard small, medium and large sizes of men's shirts.

A pull-over sweater as a concealing garment.

Bianchi "Ranger Bellyband Rig" with a S&W Chief's Special.

One example of the around-the-waist belly band holsters is the Bianchi "Ranger." The "Ranger" is designed to be worn around the waist under a concealing garment. This holster not only has a pocket to carry a handgun, but has several other pockets for carrying items ranging from small flashlights to handcuffs to spare magazines or speed loaders.

The primary advantage of belly band holsters is that they can be worn under a tucked-in shirt without sacrificing concealment. Once the shirt is tucked in, there is less loose material around the waist to effectively conceal an around-the-waist belly band, but it can still be concealed if the shirt is loose and made of heavyweight fabric. Because of this, the belly bands that are worn around the chest work better with a tucked-in shirt than the belly bands that are worn around the waist. Belly band holsters may also be worn outside of the shirt and under a zipped or buttoned lightweight jacket, like a windbreaker or warm-up jacket, but this configuration requires that you keep the jacket buttoned.

The size, body type and clothing of the individual determine how large a handgun may be carried in a belly band holster. With the chest belly bands, the handgun is carried under the weak arm. With the waist belly bands, the handgun may be carried in the middle of the waist or to one side. If the concealing garment is a jacket or heavy sweatshirt, a larger gun can be concealed.

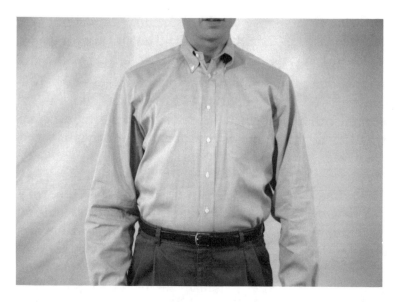

Concealed generic "Bellyband".

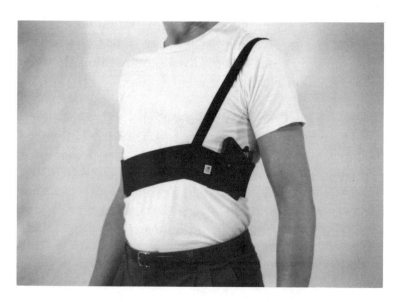

Same generic "Bellyband" with a Beretta 950 BBS over a tee shirt. Note the suspender-like strap that helps support the weight of the pistol.

Drawing from a belly band holster may or may not be a simple matter. When the belly band holster is worn under a jacket, you can simply reach into the jacket to draw the handgun. However, when a belly band holster is worn under a shirt, the difficulty of drawing the handgun is increased. To draw from a belly band holster under a shirt that does not have a button front, you must pull up the shirt and reach under the shirt tail. With a button-up shirt; you can pull up the shirt and draw from under the shirt tail, or unbutton one or more buttons and reach through the shirt to draw the handgun. It would be prohibitively slow to unbutton the shirt to draw when the gun is needed, so there are two options. First, you can go for the Elvis impersonator look and keep several buttons undone at all times for faster access. This is not always aesthetically pleasing, and it may draw unwanted attention to your shirt. The second option is to make the shirt look buttoned even when it is not. To do this, remove the strategic buttons and sew them onto the opposite side of the shirt over their corresponding button holes. Then, take small tabs of Velcro and sew them onto the shirt in place of the missing buttons to keep the shirt closed. Once this has been completed, the shirt may be pulled open quickly. A tie will also help camouflage any unbuttoned buttons or alterations.

Belly band holsters are concealable, but the size of the concealed handgun is limited. They are as easily accessed when seated as when standing. The chief disadvantage of the belly band holster is the slow speed of access, but this can be improved with the right clothes and practice. It is difficult to nonchalantly access a handgun in a belly band holster under a shirt, since pulling up a shirt or reaching into a shirt is not a common practice. I have found that when wearing a belly band holster under a shirt, it is much more comfortable to wear the holster over an undershirt and then under the concealing shirt. Like all concealing garments, dark, heavyweight shirts provide the best concealment. For some "amply bellied" or "circumferentially challenged" people, a belly band holster may not be a good choice if it is to be worn around the waist. It must be worn fairly snugly, and it compresses the lower belly and makes the "gut" move up unnaturally. To avoid this effect it must be worn around the chest.

Thunderwear Holster

The name "Thunderwear" certainly sends the imagination into high gear. However, this clever design is actually worn over the underwear and under the trousers. The Thunderwear holster is basically a pouch with a waist strap. The strap fastens around the waist and the pouch is positioned directly in front of the torso. The pouch in the holster can accommodate a medium-sized handgun and spare magazine. The pouch/holster comes in two sizes: one for tiny guns and one for medium-sized guns, in both left and right handed designs. Semi-automatic pistols work the best with Thunderwear since they typically have a slimmer profile. To draw the handgun from this holster, simply pull the trousers outward with the weak hand and grip the handgun with the strong hand.

Thunderwear is surprisingly comfortable and offers good concealment without requiring a belt. This is another holster that allows concealed carry with a shirt that is tucked into trousers. The handgun can be accessed when seated (this is extremely difficult), but it is easier to reach

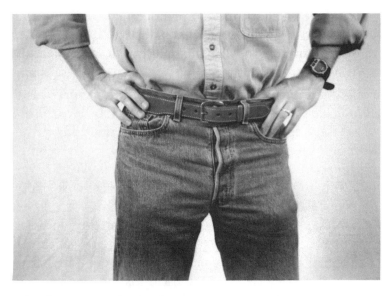

"Thunderwear" concealing a Colt Mustang.

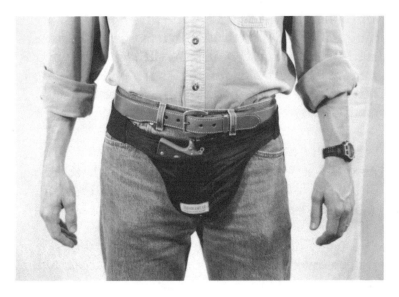

The same "Thunderwear" rig revealed.

when standing. There are two chief concerns with this type of carry. Using the restroom is a new challenge with the Thunderwear holster, and it virtually necessitates that men use a booth in public restrooms to prevent attracting unwanted attention. The second concern is a mental block; many people understandably have difficulty adapting to carrying a loaded handgun down the front of their pants. If these obstacles can be overcome, this holster is good for hot weather use or any deep cover concealment. Thunderwear works best with loose pants like sweat pants or jogging pants, but it can also work well with moderately loose jeans or slacks. The Thunderwear strap does have a tendency to ride up above the pants line in the rear, which can be visible if the Thunderwear is worn outside of a tucked-in shirt. This can be solved in two ways; either do not tuck in your shirt or wear a shirt that has the sides split at the bottom. This allows the back of the shirt to be worn outside of the holster and the front worn under the holster. I have a friend who swears by this arrangement and modifies his shirts to better accommodate the Thunderwear. As you will see in the "Access Time of Various Concealed Carry Modes" section, Thunderwear can provide respectable access time with practice.

Hollow Belt Accessory Holsters

There are at least two types of hollow belt accessory holsters: hollow pager cases and hollow "Walkman"-type belt radios/cassette players. The basic idea is that a mini-revolver, autoloader or derringer can be concealed inside a fake belt radio or pager. These hollow electronics have a hinged cover that swings open to provide access to the tiny gun stashed inside.

Seer hollow "Pager Holster".

Seer "Pager Holster" opened to reveal a Davis Industries derringer.

This type of holster has many disadvantages and few advantages. Some of these hollow electronics are cheaply built and do not look authentic under even mild scrutiny. They are so small that they can accommodate only the tiniest of handguns, and this type of holster is slow to draw from. The belt radio may be the target of a mugger, and the hollow pager is suspiciously larger than most modern belt pagers. The advantage of this type of holster is that it can blend in and look normal from a distance. The bottom line is that there are other holsters that can better meet the targeted need of these hollow cases. The tiny guns that can be concealed in these devices can be more conveniently and effectively carried in a pocket holster.

Jacket Holsters

There are several garments on the market that have hidden pockets that serve as holsters. One example is the Spiewak "Hidden Agenda" line of garments, consisting of denim or "jean" jackets, windbreaker-type jackets, and vests. These jackets have deep slash pockets just inside each lapel that can serve as holsters. The pistol can be accessed by reaching across the chest into the pocket, a motion similar to accessing a shoulder holster. An advantage for professionals is that these jackets have hidden tabs on the front and back that can be pulled down to reveal identifier flaps with "POLICE," "SECURITY," "FIRE," "EMS," or "SHERIFF" printed in bold white letters against a dark background. These jackets are of sufficient length to conceal an IWB holster and also have internal shoulder pads to help support the weight of your gear. The hidden pocket can be fastened with the Velcro closure for a more secure carry. This pocket can serve as a holster in a pinch, but without a good pocket holster it is not an adequate full-time replacement for a dedicated holster.

The advantages of this type of jacket are the identifier flaps (for professionals only) and the versatility of the "holster pocket." Many sizes of handguns may be carried in this pocket without other holsters if absolutely necessary. This jacket offers exceptional concealment of the handgun when the gun is carried in the closed holster pocket. This jacket can also be a good alternative to a large pocketed overcoat that is used to carry a full-sized handgun. Consider this scenario: you are carrying an IWB or shoulder holster that is concealed by a jacket, so the jacket cannot be removed without exposing the handgun. The concealing jacket may have felt great outside in the cold, but once you get indoors you become uncomfortably warm. You are stuck wearing the jacket since it is concealing your IWB holster. With the Hidden Agenda jacket, you could carry your gun in the holster pocket and remove your jacket without exposing your handgun. The handgun could not be rapidly accessed, but it would be much closer than if it were in your locked automobile. However, a danger is forgetting about the handgun and leaving the jacket unattended, even if only to go to the restroom.

Disadvantages of this jacket include the relatively slow access to the handgun and the tendency of the gun to shift position in the large holster pocket. This may cause some fumbling and more lost time while you are finding your firing grip on the gun. The jacket will sag a little on the side that is supporting the handgun unless it is weight balanced. This is easy enough to do since each side of the jacket has an interior pocket that can hold a counterweight. This carry method is useless for warm weather, since the jacket is the holster.

"Hidden Agenda" denim jacket.

"Hidden Agenda" jacket with the front identifier and badge flaps pulled down.

"Hidden Agenda" jacket with the rear identifier flap pulled down.

"Hidden Agenda" jacket interior slash pocket with a Colt Mustang in a K.L. Null "Side Pocket Scabbard".

This jacket superbly fills a specific niche, but it should not routinely replace a good holster as a primary carry option. The "POLICE" identifiers are tremendously useful to officers, and this is the most important feature of the jacket.

Other Miscellaneous Carry

There are countless other modes of concealed carry, and many do not even use holsters. I have seen all types of makeshift "holsters" constructed from elastic bands fastened around the waist, chest or legs. A tiny revolver can be concealed in the rolled-up fold of a stocking cap, and the same gun can be concealed worn around the neck on a lanyard. Tiny guns may also be concealed in custom boot holsters, or even in the palm of one hand under a pair of winter gloves or mittens. While these methods may provide effective concealment, there are other more conventional options that will usually work better.

One other carry option worth mentioning is the bib pocket of overalls. Most working/farming types of overalls have a bib pocket that can be closed with a zipper. This pocket can serve as a large holster pocket similar to the one in a Hidden Agenda jacket. The pocket may be worn with the zipper open and the handgun will still be concealed fairly well, unless the wearer is unusually short. Another customized option is to sew a holster or pouch into the interior of the bib on the overalls. This way the handgun can be casually accessed by reaching behind the bib. Although this may sound like something from Hee Haw, it works. However, you must remember your surroundings. You do not want your concealing garments to draw attention to yourself, and overalls are not appropriate in a five-star restaurant (unless you are as rich as Jed Clampett). Still, in areas where overalls are common, this is an inexpensive and secure way to conceal a handgun.

Ultimately, there are many creative ways to effectively conceal a handgun; you just need to find the combination which works best for you.

Chapter 6
CONCEALED CARRY HOLSTERS FOR WOMEN

The vast majority of people who carry concealed hand-guns are men, thus there is a wider variety of conceal-ment holsters offered for men than for women. However, in recent years women have been obtaining CCW permits in record numbers. With more women carrying concealed handguns, the market for women's concealment holsters should improve. Still, a wide selection of women's con-cealment holsters is presently available.

The obvious anatomical differences between men and women must be considered when choosing women's concealment holsters. Women tend to be higher-waisted than men; i.e. women's torsos make up a smaller fraction of their total height than men's torsos. In addition, women are generally shorter than men. Women also tend to be more hourglass-shaped than men, in other words the relative difference between the hip and waist dimensions is usually greater for women than men.

Belt Holsters
The above mentioned factors combine to present prob-lems when women use belt holsters that were designed for men. One good example is a high-ride belt holster that was designed for a man. With this holster, the average

man can comfortably reach the grip of the handgun to draw the gun. On many women, this configuration places the grip of the handgun nearly under the armpit, causing obvious comfort and access problems. Because women's hips curve in at the top more than men's, many belt holsters designed for men cause the gun butt to dig into the ribs when worn by women.

This problem has been solved by several major holster designers. Greg Kramer of Kramer Leather has designed a belt scabbard holster specifically for women. Mr. Kramer's "Women's Belt Scabbard" holster carries the gun lower on the belt than typical belt scabbards. The belt slot is lined with molded plastic that causes the gun butt to tilt slightly away from the body. These two deviations from typical scabbard holsters prevent the grip from digging into the side and keep the butt from being so high under the arm. This holster is made of horsehide leather and carries the gun with an FBI tilt.

Gould and Goodrich sells a holster called the "Lady Body Guard." This holster consists of a wide elastic belt with an elastic slot style holster and spare magazine pouch. The belt has a fashionably large buckle that comes in red or brown, while the belt is available in black or tan. This belt/holster combination is designed to be worn under a sweater or blazer, with pants or a skirt.

Bruce Nelson Combat Leather (Mr. Nelson was the original designer of the legendary "Summer Special" IWB holster) offers a "Woman's Holster Adapter." This device is a padded foam spacer that is designed to be worn between the pants and blouse behind a strong side scabbard holster. This adapter positions the gun so that the butt does not dig into the wearer's side, allowing a smoother draw.

Concealed Colt Mustang in a Kramer "IWB #2" holster.

Colt Mustang in a Kramer "IWB #2" holster.

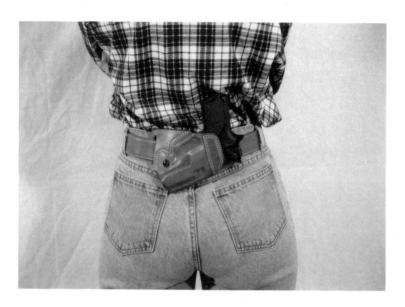

Galco "SOB" holster for a S&W 3913. Note the tension adjustment screw.

As discussed earlier, Small of the Back (SOB) holsters work for women as well as men, and the advantages and disadvantages of this type of holster are listed in Chapter 2. Since women do not wear belts as frequently as men, the Paddle holsters of Chapter 2 are also of interest to many women. These holsters do not require a belt, so they can be effectively worn with a skirt as well as slacks.

Holster Purses

A traditional place for a woman to carry a handgun is in her purse, but there are several tactical problems with this mode of carry. First, items other than the handgun are usually carried loose in the purse as well. This presents difficulties in rapidly acquiring a firing grip on the handgun. If you are reaching for your gun amid an assortment of keys, checkbook, wallet, et cetera, chances are that you will have difficulty in quickly achieving your firing grip. Furthermore, a handgun carried loose in a purse is subject to being inadvertently revealed any time the purse is opened in public. A loose handgun is also exposed to debris/lint from the purse that may cause reliability problems.

These problems are remedied with a good holster purse. Most holster purses are designed with a separate compartment for the handgun, usually accessible through a zipper or a Velcro-type closure that looks like a seam on the purse. Inside the holster compartment the gun is typically secured in a nylon, leather or neoprene holster. This insures that the handgun is properly positioned at all times. Many holster purses have a cut resistant shoulder strap to help prevent purse snatchings. In some models, the wearer may keep one hand inside the holster compartment with a firing grip on the handgun without looking conspicuous. This option dramatically increases the accessibility of the handgun.

The advantages of a holster purse are many. A large handgun can be effectively concealed by a small woman who could not conceal the same gun in a conventional holster. A purse is appropriate for any occasion, and with the wide variety of holster purses available, different ones can be purchased for different situations. With the many different models of holster purses on the market, the chance of one being recognized as a holster purse is slim. In this respect, holster purses have the advantage of being less conspicuous than the popular holster fanny packs. A firing grip can be obtained on the handgun in most holster purses without telegraphing the action, greatly increasing

Guardian Leather "Holster Purse" with wrist strap that attaches to the grip of the concealed handgun.

Same Guardian Leather purse with wrist strap attached to a Colt Detective Special.

access speed. If you refer to the "Access Time of Various Concealed Carry Modes" section, you will see that the access time for a holster purse when a firing grip is already obtained is very fast. Holster purses do not require a concealing garment, so the same handgun/purse combination can be used for all seasons and temperature ranges. In an emergency, the handgun may be crudely pointed and fired through the purse without being drawn from the purse. Because of this, revolvers are often chosen as holster purse handguns (instead of semi-automatics.) A revolver, particularly with a concealed, shrouded, or bobbed hammer, would be much more reliable when fired while still inside the purse. With a semi-automatic, the action of the slide and the ejection of spent casings would most likely cause the handgun to jam if fired while inside the holster compartment of a purse. The greatest advantage of the holster purse is convenience; these purses afford probably the most hassle-free mode of concealed carry for a full-sized handgun.

An additional advantage of holster purses is that if you use different purses and the same gun as your sole concealed carry mode for various occasions, you are following Bianchi's Law (See Chapter 1) of one gun and one mode of carry. This has the advantage of requiring training for one mode of carry only. When you follow Bianchi's Law, you have a better chance of instinctively drawing and firing your defensive handgun quickly and effectively under high stress conditions.

As with any concealed carry mode, the holster purse has its disadvantages. Most importantly, the handgun is not worn on the body with a holster purse, which means that if the purse is separated from you then so is your handgun.

Additionally, a holster purse may draw the attention of a purse snatcher, but this problem is partially solved by the many models that offer shoulder straps containing cut-resistant steel cables. Holster purses offer relatively slow access to the handgun unless you have already obtained a firing grip, since the purse is not affixed to your person like a conventional holster. However, Guardian Leather is one company that offers a solution to this problem. Guardian Leather sells a holster purse that comes with a leather wrist loop that has Velcro straps on the end of it. These straps fasten around the grip of your handgun. When you put your gun in the purse and fasten the Velcro seam, the wrist loop is left sticking out of the purse. To draw the gun, simply grab the wrist loop and pull the gun out of the purse. With practice, this can be fairly fast. (See the access times in Chapter 7.) This is good insurance against a purse snatcher. If you have your wrist through the loop, even if your purse is snatched your gun will conveniently come out in your hand.

It is a good idea to shop around before buying a holster purse. As you shop, look for one that is designed so you can nonchalantly achieve a firing grip on the handgun without revealing your actions. Additionally, they come in enough styles to please even the most discriminating consumer, so it's not necessary to buy on impulse. For example, Lady B Safe offers three styles of holster purses in eight colors. Feminine Protection offers over 30 styles in ten colors and 20 sizes made in two different materials (leather or denim); that amounts to over 500 possible combinations. One word of advice for the guys who are contemplating buying a holster purse for ANY female: wife, sister, girlfriend, mother or daughter as a gift or surprise. STOP RIGHT THERE! Do not buy a holster purse without consulting the person who will use the purse. I am convinced that men are cosmically clueless about "handbag fashion." (I found this out the hard way - With my wife and both sisters!) To a guy, a purse should be useful; you know - huge, indestructible, with two shoulder straps like a backpack and preferably made out of some good sturdy material like angle-iron. Women are very specific about the types of purses they like, and many women would rather leave their guns at home than carry the "wrong" purse.

Purse/Briefcase Inserts

Similar in concept, purse/briefcase inserts are available from several manufacturers. These inserts are typically designed to snap or Velcro into the purse or briefcase. The actual insert functions like a snap-in holster. These inserts have the advantage of being workable in several different accessories; the same insert can be used in a variety of purses and briefcases. Inserts offer many of the same advantages as holster purses. They can accommodate large handguns, they are convenient, they do not require a concealing garment, and they can be appropriate for nearly any occasion in the proper handbag. Also, inserts offer the flexibility of being used in multiple accessories, and they are significantly less expensive than holster purses.

The disadvantages of inserts include poor accessibility and inability to casually obtain a firing grip. Such a grip cannot always be obtained nonchalantly with an insert, because the insert is simply carried inside the purse. Inserts also have the same negatives as carrying a handgun loose in a conventional purse; the handgun is not in a separate compartment, thus, it is surrounded by other items in the purse. The handgun may be fouled with debris and lint from the purse, and the handgun is likely to be inadvertently exposed when the purse is opened in public. The access problem is even worse if the insert is inside a closed briefcase.

Holster purses are an attractive option for concealed carry, and they are probably worth the extra money versus a purse insert.

Thigh Holsters

Several manufacturers, including Galco and Feminine Protection, offer thigh or garter belt holsters. These holsters consist of a holster band worn around the thigh and a waist belt that has a strap connecting to the holster band. The waist belt is designed to help support the weight of the handgun and the holster band via the connecting strap. The holster often has a Velcro thumb break or strap to retain the gun. These holsters are best used with small to medium handguns and are most effectively concealed with a fairly loose skirt or dress.

Thigh holsters are similar to ankle holsters in the respect that some people have difficulty getting accustomed to the additional weight of a handgun on one leg, though this problem is not as severe as with ankle holsters because the weight is further up the leg. The advantages of thigh holsters include good concealment with the proper clothes; for example a small woman can conceal a medium-sized gun effectively with a thigh holster and appropriate concealing dress or skirt. A thigh holster can be used effectively with no additional concealing garment like a blazer or jacket, so a handgun may be concealed with only a light summer dress or skirt and no purse.

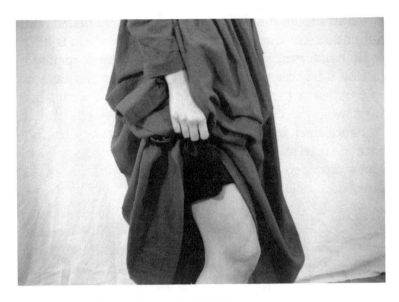

Galco "Thigh Holster" with a Beretta 950 BBS.

On the downside, thigh holsters can chew up nylon panty hose, and many people find them uncomfortable. The access to a handgun in a thigh holster is slow, and there is no way to casually achieve a firing grip without looking like an exhibitionist. A thigh holster is very difficult to access when seated if a long dress or skirt is worn, and large handguns are difficult to carry in this mode.

Other Traditional Modes of Concealed Carry

All the traditional modes of carry that men use can also be used for women. Ankle holsters, shoulder holsters, pocket holsters and accessory holsters may be employed for women. Women's slacks tend to have more taper on the legs, so ankle holster handguns and concealment clothes need to be carefully considered. Large chested women may find shoulder holsters uncomfortable to draw from, and pocket holsters are still an attractive alternative for small handguns. Accessory holsters, especially fanny pack holsters, offer great handgun concealment for women. (In fact, fanny packs were first worn in non-sporting use by women who used the convenient packs as substitutes for handbags.) Because of this, there is not the lingering trace of social stigma for women who use fanny packs as opposed to men who use them. The pros and cons of the fanny pack holster are discussed at length in Chapter 4.

Concealment Clothing for Women

In general, concealment clothing for women follows the same principles as for men. Each chapter on different holsters offers suggestion for concealment clothing. However, since women tend to be smaller framed than men, the same gun takes a little more effort to conceal on a woman. One company that has recognized this problem is PistolERA. PistolERA offers a line of women's clothing that is designed and custom made for handgun concealment. Adjustable inserts are sewn into the slacks and shirts that are designed to support the weight of a handgun, and these clothes can be worn with or without a handgun. Bloused jackets are available for shoulder holster or belt holster carry. Since the clothing is custom made, both the appropriate measurements and mode of carry must be specified when an order is placed. This clothing line includes jackets, vests, slacks and skirts offered in cotton/poly blends, linen, silk, wools and gabardines.

Final Thoughts

One suggestion is to carry a holster purse in your automobile at all times, in the event that some emergency causes you to leave the relative safety of your vehicle. Many women do not routinely carry a handgun for self defense, but they do keep one in their automobile. A holster purse will give these women an uncomplicated, discreet method of concealed carry that is far superior to simply stuffing the gun into a standard purse if they are forced to leave their car. Now, one response to this suggestion may be "I've got a cellular phone, so I won't need to leave my car." This reasoning contains several fallacies. There are still many areas that do not have cellular coverage, and cellular phone batteries and car batteries may lose their charge. A cellular phone may also experience some other malfunction, whether from an auto accident or general equipment failure. A cellular phone is a valuable part of your personal security plan, but do not place too much faith in it. To continue this line of thought, a cellular phone alone is no substitute for a defensive handgun in an automobile. If you are stranded in an area inhabited by trolls (which is, unfortunately, more and more common,) a cellular phone cannot provide the immediate protection that you might need. Therefore, a cellular phone is no replacement for a defensive sidearm and your competency with the sidearm.

Chapter 7
ACCESS TIMES OF VARIOUS
CONCEALED CARRY MODES

One of the key factors in choosing a concealment holster or mode of concealed carry is access to the handgun. Remember that concealed carry of a handgun should be a happy balance of concealment, power (caliber), capacity, access and comfort. You will need to experiment with different holsters, handguns and modes of carry to determine how comfortable and concealable each combination is for you. Because accessibility is crucial for self-defense, no discussion of concealed carry would be complete without a comparison of access times for different carry modes.

The data in this chapter was compiled from the results of four different shooters of widely varying abilities. As a reference, Shooter A is a former A-Class IPSC (International Practical Shooting Confederation) shooter and Bianchi Cup competitor; Shooter B is a novice IPSC shooter; Shooter C is a self-defense/recreational shooter; and Shooter D is a self-defense shooter who has only been shooting for 9 months. The intent of this chapter is not to see what the best time is, but to show the relative access speeds of different modes of concealed carry for different individuals. The data was collected as follows: for each different mode of carry the shooter stood at a distance of seven yards from the target, with arms relaxed. The shooter stood facing the target with the handgun concealed. The start signal was the beep from a PACT Club timer, a handy audible timer that automatically stops the clock when the shot is fired. At the signal, the shooter drew and fired one shot at the target as rapidly and accurately as possible. Each shot had to hit the standard IPSC target, a roughly humanoid cardboard target, in order to count. The time for each shot was then recorded. The time was measured from the start signal of the timer until the "bang" of the shot, so the reaction time of the shooter is included (usually about .20-.25 seconds for good reflexes) as well as the time it takes to access and present the handgun. Each shooter fired ten separate times from each carry mode. These ten times were averaged to give the access time for each mode. The result is a rough picture of how accessible the various modes of concealed carry are. For comparison, several modes were also timed starting with a firing grip on the handgun. This demonstrates the access time advantage of modes of carry that offer a casual firing grip. All times shown are in seconds.

Even though only one of the shooters was female, all of the shooters tried the holster purse. These times are the result of minimal practice, since men have no need to practice with a holster purse. (It was difficult enough to get the men to shoot with the purse, much less practice with it!)

You will also note that only one participant used the Thunderwear. The rest of the shooters were, shall we say, gun-shy, at the prospect of using the Thunderwear without extensive dry-fire practice. Shooter C had been dry-fire practicing for weeks with the Thunderwear. It should also be noted that Shooter C is left-handed and the Thunderwear used was the right-handed model; he felt that he could improve his respectable Thunderwear access times even more with the left-handed version.

The pocket holster was carried in an exterior coat pocket by each shooter. If the pocket holster had been in a pants pocket instead, the access times would have been slower. A large exterior coat pocket typically offers the fastest access for a pocket rig.

Two different types of fanny packs were used, a Guardian Leather Velcro-fastened fanny pack used by Shooter A and a zipper-fastened Bianchi pack used by the other shooters. Many people will argue that the Velcro-type fastened packs offer faster access. However, the fanny pack access times for Shooters A and B suggest that this is not necessarily so. Shooter A is faster than Shooter B in every category, including the fanny pack, but the difference between their fanny pack access times is consistent with the difference between the rest of their times. The data indicates that there is no significant access time difference between Velcro type fastened packs and zipper fastened packs, provided that the user has practiced sufficiently.

Two types of holster purses were also used, a generic over-the-shoulder model and a Guardian Leather purse that has an external wrist loop (see Chapter 6) fastened to the grip of the concealed handgun. Note the access times of Shooters C and D. Shooter C has faster times in every area except when using the holster purse with the hands relaxed. In this case, it is obvious that the exterior wrist loop of the Guardian Leather purse offers faster access than the generic purse.

Shooter A

Mode	Holster	Gun	Hands Relaxed	Firing Grip
IWB	Rogers Crossdraw	Colt Lightweight Commander	1.27	0.74
Scabbard	Bianchi-Askins Aveng.	Colt Lightweight Commander	1.49	1.21
Pocket	K.L. Null - SPS	Colt Mustang Nite Lite	2.03	0.73
Shoulder	Rogers	S&W 3913	1.41	
Fanny Pack	Guardian Leather	S&W Chief's Special	1.68	
Purse	Guardian Leather	S&W Chief's Special	1.55	0.92

Shooter B

Mode	Holster	Gun	Hands Relaxed	Firing Grip
IWB	M. Sparks-Ex. Comp.	Firestar M-40	1.77	0.93
Scabbard	Bianchi-Askins Aveng.	Browning High Power	1.71	
Pocket	K.L. Null - SPS	Colt Mustang Nite Lite	2.50	1.47
Shoulder	DeSantis - Slant	Firestar M-40	2.05	1.23
Fanny Pack	Bianchi - KO	Browning High Power	2.01	
Purse	Guardian Leather	Charter Arms Off Duty	2.19	1.02

Shooter C

Mode	Holster	Gun	Hands Relaxed	Firing Grip
IWB	Galco - NSA	Beretta 92FS	1.81	1.27
Scabbard	Safariland Paddle	Beretta 92FS	1.99	
Pocket	K.L. Null - SPS	Colt Mustang Nite Lite	2.57	1.57
Shoulder	DeSantis - Slant	Firestar M-40	2.58	1.19
Fanny Pack	Bianchi - KO	Browning High Power	2.23	
Purse	Generic	Colt Detective Special	2.95	1.14
Thunderwear	Thunderwear	Grendel P10	2.05	

Shooter D

Mode	Holster	Gun	Hands Relaxed	Firing Grip
IWB	M. Sparks-Ex. Comp.	Firestar M-40	2.35	1.43
Scabbard	Bianchi-Askins Aveng.	Browning High Power	2.17	
Pocket	K.L. Null - SPS	Colt Mustang Nite Lite	2.74	1.92
Shoulder	DeSantis - Slant	Firestar M-40	2.91	1.73
Fanny Pack	Bianchi - KO	Browning High Power	2.89	
Purse	Guardian Leather	Charter Arms Off Duty	2.72	1.93

* All times shown are in seconds.

Chapter 8
CONCLUSION

There is a great responsibility that goes along with carrying a concealed firearm. Everyone who "carries" owes it to himself and his fellow citizens to read the book *In the Gravest Extreme - The Role of the Firearm in Personal Protection* by Massad Ayoob. Then read it again. Mr. Ayoob is a distinguished police officer, author of several books, Contributing Editor of several popular gun magazines, champion pistol shot and expert on the use of lethal force. Mr. Ayoob has penned an excellent text that goes far beyond advice on what type of gun to carry. *In the Gravest Extreme* discusses at length the philosophy of carrying a gun for self protection and the ramifications of having to use that gun. This book should be required reading for anyone who has a CCW permit. Do not be discouraged by the 1980 copyright date on this book; the information in it is timeless. Consider this brief excerpt from Chapter 11: "Common Sense About Carrying Guns".

> *The man who wears a gun carries with it the power of life and death, and therefore the responsibility to deport himself with greater*

*calm and wisdom than his unarmed coun-
terpart, whose panic or misjudgment in
crisis situations will have less serious con-
sequences. The power of the gun is never
ignored, no matter how accustomed one
becomes to the weight on his hip. A man
carrying a gun for the first time is acutely,
even uncomfortably aware of its presence.
After a time, he ceases to notice both the
weight and the responsibility, not because
he has forgotten them, but because they
have both been assimilated into his bearing
and demeanor. (p. 81)*

When you carry a concealed handgun, it should remain
just that: CONCEALED. It is bad form to display or reveal
your concealed handgun frivolously, not to mention poor
strategy. While the right to keep and bear arms is inalienable, concealed carry is a privilege. Citizens legally armed
with a CCW should not abuse or jeopardize this privilege
by unnecessarily "showing their piece."

Before legally carrying a concealed handgun, you should
become competent with the firearm that you will carry.
This does not mean simply learning to shoot the handgun
proficiently; you should practice drawing and shooting
from concealment. First, practice this dry, and after you
have mastered that, go to live ammunition. Keep safety
foremost in mind as you practice. Do not strive for speed,
but for smoothness and accuracy. Speed will come with
time, but do not sacrifice accuracy for speed. A fast miss
isn't much of a deterrent to a criminal attacker.

An excellent way to develop competency under stressful conditions is to compete. The stress of competition does not approximate the stress of a lethal encounter, but competitive shooting does produce more stress than simple plinking. The more that you are able to practice the better, and some forms of competitive shooting still have enough practical elements to be beneficial. During practical (IPSC type) or action shooting competition, you are likely to run into some problems that you may encounter on the street: shooting weak-handed, shooting from awkward positions, shoot/no-shoot decisions, shooting as fast and accurately as possible and dealing with equipment problems. If you do participate in organized shooting, keep your equipment practical. Much of the competitors' gear that you see at matches would never be carried on the street; it is too bulky to be concealed without great difficulty. Compete with your carry gun and holster occasionally at least, and keep your "match gun" practical.

Mindset is as important as the weapon itself. Remember the old saying that "an ounce of prevention is worth a pound of cure." Use your mental alertness to keep you out of situations that may escalate into a lethal confrontation. Trouble is not always avoidable, so if you can't avoid it, be prepared for it. Learn about Jeff Cooper's conditions of mental alertness (paraphrased from his outstanding book, *Fireworks*):

Condition White   Unalert, unarmed, will be completely surprised and probably die if attacked.

Condition Yellow	Alert, aware of surroundings. Yellow must be assumed when armed - It is possible to remain in Yellow indefinitely without undue nervous strain.
Condition Orange	Alerted to some immediate danger, a state of alarm with reason to believe that a fight is likely. Careful not to over-react while keeping back covered. A controlled shot should be available with about three seconds' notice.
Condition Red	"All systems are GO." If you see a deadly threat you shoot, and a controlled shot is available in about one second.

Making the decision to carry a concealed handgun is a significant paradigm shift for most people. It means you realize that self protection is ultimately the responsibility of the individual. Once you have drawn this conclusion, you understand that competency and discretion with your carry gun is crucially important. You would not consider carrying a gun with which you are not sufficiently trained. You also carry your gun without a second thought, as naturally as you carry your wallet or purse. In fact, once you have developed this mindset, you feel uncomfortable without your carry gun, painfully aware that you are vulnerable.

This book would not be complete without a list of my favorite carry combinations. This is not an endorsement, but these are the combinations that I have found to work best for me. My primary carry rig is the compact Star Firestar M-40 in a Milt Sparks "Executives Companion" IWB holster. This combination is worn with either a Galco "1 1/2 inch Contour" belt or the Galco 1 1/4 inch "Firm System" contour dress belt. This rig is usually concealed with an untucked rugby or golf shirt, a sports coat, a sweater, a down vest or a Banana Republic safari vest. For concealed carry in tourist areas or for day hiking, I carry the Firestar in a Bianchi K.O. fanny pack. I am also a fan of pocket carry, and my favorite pocket rig is a Colt Mustang Nite Lite in a pocket holster by either Greg Kramer or Kenneth L. Null. The Nite Lite's weight (13 ounces) makes it perfect for pocket carry. The Null pocket holster is wider than the Kramer holster, so I prefer it for large coat pockets (especially my Hidden Agenda interior coat pocket). The smaller Kramer holster is better suited for trouser or shorts pocket carry. Both the Firestar and the Colt are equipped with tritium night sights.

Hopefully this book has helped you sort through the various concealed carry options without unnecessary expense. Good luck in your search for concealment holsters, and I hope you will never be forced to use your CCW. Remember, practice drawing and shooting from concealment, and stay alert! Your greatest asset lies between your ears.

BIBLIOGRAPHY

Ayoob, Massad F., *In the Gravest Extreme.* Concord, N.H.: Police Bookshelf, 1980

Bianchi, John, *Bluesteel & Gunleather.* North Hollywood, CA.: Beinfeld Publishing, 1978

Cooper, Jeff, *Fireworks.* Paulden, AZ.: Gunsite Press, 1989

Cooper, Jeff, *The Gargantuan Gunsite Gossip.* Paulden, AZ.: Gunsite Press, 1990

Cooper, Jeff, *Principles of Personal Defense.* Boulder, CO.: Paladin Press, 1972

Federal Bureau of Investigation, "Crime in the United States", 1994

Gratia, Suzanna, testimony given before the Texas House Public Safety Committee, February 18, 1993

Jordan, Bill, *No Second Place Winner.* Shreveport, LA.: Bill Jordan, 1965

Kleck, Gary, *Point Blank: Guns and Violence in America.* New York, N.Y.: Aldine de Gruyter, 1991

LaPierre, Wayne, *Guns, Crime and Freedom.* Washington, D.C.: Regnery Publishing, 1994

Levinson, Sanford, "The Embarrassing Second Amendment," 99 Yale Law Journal, 1989

Quigley, Paxton, *Armed & Female.* New York, N.Y.: Viking Penguin, 1989

Wright, James D. & Rossi, Peter H., *The Armed Criminal in America: A Survey of Incarcerated Felons,* U.S. Department of Justice, National Institute of Justice, July 1985

Warren v. District of Columbia, D.C. App., 444 A. 2d 1, 1981

APPENDIX

This is a list of all makers of concealed carry products known to the author. Prices are current as of early 1995. While every effort was made to ensure the accuracy and completeness of this list, mistakes and omissions may have occurred, so write or call for a current catalog before ordering. It is customary to include two or three dollars with a catalog request to defray printing and postage costs.

A&J Police Equipment 7616 Third Avenue Brooklyn, NY 11209 (718) 833-5535	*IWB*	*Shoulder*	*Purse*	*Women's*	*Ankle*	*Fanny Pack*	*Scabbard*	*Pocket*
Price Range:	$21 -35				$32		$35 -39	
Sells Cobra Gunskin leather holsters. Also sells a black bellyband-type rig for $27.								

Ace Case Co. 1530 Pheasant Ridge Ellisville, MO 63011 (800) 544-0008	*IWB*	*Shoulder*	*Purse*	*Women's*	*Ankle*	*Fanny Pack*	*Scabbard*	*Pocket*
Price Range:	$13 -18	$23 -30			$20	$20		

Makes nylon holsters, accessories, and gun cases. A few holsters are available for guns with lasers or scopes. Also sells a bellyband-type rig for $20.

Ahern Enterprises, Inc. P.O. Box 186 Commerce, GA 30529 (800) 285-1245	*IWB*	*Shoulder*	*Purse*	*Women's*	*Ankle*	*Fanny Pack*	*Scabbard*	*Pocket*
Price Range:	$47	$70 -110		$61	$70		$47	

Ahern Enterprises (Jerry Ahern the gun writer's company) sells several more-or-less traditional nylon holsters that can be carried in a variety of ways (shoulder, belt, etc.). However, he also sells some far from traditional concealable rigs that can be attached beneath your outer garments. One of these is designed specifically for women. He also carries a rig for hiding guns in unusual places like under tables or above your auto's sun visor. This catalog is a must if you are exploring "deep concealment" options.

Aker Leather Products 2248 Main St., Suite 6 Chula Vista, CA 91911-3932 (619) 423-1363	*IWB*	*Shoulder*	*Purse*	*Women's*	*Ankle*	*Fanny Pack*	*Scabbard*	*Pocket*
Price Range:	$12 -13	$76 -82				$46	$26 -36	$18

Leather duty and concealment products. Sells a unique back-up holster that attaches to a bulletproof vest.

Alessi Holsters, Inc. 2465 Niagara Falls Blvd. Amherst, NY 14228-3527 (716) 691-5615	*IWB*	*Shoulder*	*Purse*	*Women's*	*Ankle*	*Fanny Pack*	*Scabbard*	*Pocket*
Price Range:	$30 -55	$85 -120			$60		$50 -55	$30

Alessi's custom shop makes molded, hand boned holsters at a reasonable price. The Alessi "Talon" IWB rig is one of the best "clip" style IWB holsters available.

Bagmaster Mfg. Inc. 2731 Sutton Ave. St. Louis, MO 63143 (800) 950-8181	*IWB*	*Shoulder*	*Purse*	*Women's*	*Ankle*	*Fanny Pack*	*Scabbard*	*Pocket*
Price Range:	$16 -18	$32 -35			$20	$16 -26	$16 -18	

Nylon holsters and fanny packs (along with rifle and pistol cases). Sells several holsters for guns with lasers or scopes attached.

Barami Corporation 6689 Orchard Lake Rd. #148 West Bloomfield, MI 48322 (810) 738-0462	*IWB*	*Shoulder*	*Purse*	*Women's*	*Ankle*	*Fanny Pack*	*Scabbard*	*Pocket*
Price Range:								

Barami sells a unique item: the "Hip-Grip." This is a replacement grip for revolvers that has a "lip" on it to keep the gun in place when inserted into the waistband. Sort of a "holsterless" holster. The gun can still be gripped and fired normally. The "Hip Grip" costs $18.95 and is available for most popular revolvers.

Bianchi International 100 Calle Cortez Temecula, CA 92590 (800) 477-8545 Catalog $3	*IWB*	*Shoulder*	*Purse*	*Women's*	*Ankle*	*Fanny Pack*	*Scabbard*	*Pocket*
Price Range:	$10 -58	$58 -109			$35 -60	$52	$40 -75	

Founded by concealed-carry expert and holster-designer John Bianchi. Bianchi makes leather and nylon holsters in a wide variety of styles. Their "Accumold" line of nylon holsters is molded to fit the shape of the gun that they are designed for. They carry a bellyband rig for $28. They also make strip ammo loaders; a slim (though slower) alternative to speedloaders for revolvers. Bianchi products are widely available in sporting goods and gun stores.

Ted Blocker Holsters, Inc. 5360 N.E. 112th Portland, OR 97220 (503) 254-9950	*IWB*	*Shoulder*	*Purse*	*Women's*	*Ankle*	*Fanny Pack*	*Scabbard*	*Pocket*
Price Range:	$17 -105	$85 -112					$37 -51	

Sells several leather scabbards and IWB holsters. One of their offerings is the LFI IWB rig, which was designed in collaboration with Massad Ayoob. It can be adjusted to any desired degree of cant.

Boyt Sporting Goods Division 509 Hamilton Iowa Falls, Iowa 50126 (515) 648-2058	*IWB*	*Shoulder*	*Purse*	*Women's*	*Ankle*	*Fanny Pack*	*Scabbard*	*Pocket*
Price Range:			$180 -200			$52		

Boyt carries the Paxton Quigley (author of *Armed and Female*) Signature Line of women's shooting equipment. This consists of purses, fanny packs, briefcases, and handgun cases.

Brauer Bros. Mfg. Co. 2020 Delmar St. Louis, MO 63103 (314) 231-2864	IWB	Shoulder	Purse	Women's	Ankle	Fanny Pack	Scabbard	Pocket
Price Range:	$5 -13	$35 -54			$18 -24		$18 -32	

Leather and nylon holsters and accessories. Left-handed holsters are available, but cost 10% extra.

C.C. Mfg. Co. 16161 Nordhoff St. #242 North Hills, CA 91343	IWB	Shoulder	Purse	Women's	Ankle	Fanny Pack	Scabbard	Pocket
Price Range:								$25

Sells the "Deprinter", a gizmo that attaches to your pocket pistol to break up its outline in your pocket, and hold the gun in a consistent position. The device is drawn out with the gun. Fits most small guns, will be custom made for yours if necessary.

Chester and Company P.O. Box 2402 Hollister, CA 95024 (408) 637-1157	IWB	Shoulder	Purse	Women's	Ankle	Fanny Pack	Scabbard	Pocket
Price Range:								

Sells the "Companion" line of hollow electronics. These devices are worn on the belt, and can conceal a derringer or small autoloader. They could also carry defense sprays, alarms, etc. all of which are also available from Chester and Co. The units may be purchased with a clock and FM radio.

Coronado Leather 120 C Avenue Coronado, CA 92118 (619) 435-1869	IWB	Shoulder	Purse	Women's	Ankle	Fanny Pack	Scabbard	Pocket
Price Range:			$78 -93			$50 -60		

Sells leather purses, fanny packs, bags, and briefcases with integral pistol pouches.

D.B. Southwest Leather, Co. P.O. Box 1857 Lakeside, CA 92040 (800) 706-8524	IWB	Shoulder	Purse	Women's	Ankle	Fanny Pack	Scabbard	Pocket
Price Range:			$58 -70			$50 -60		

Leather holster purses and fanny packs, in a variety of styles and colors.

DeSantis Holster & Leather Goods 149 Denton Ave. New Hyde Park, NY 11040 (516) 354-8000 Catalog $3	IWB	Shoulder	Purse	Women's	Ankle	Fanny Pack	Scabbard	Pocket
Price Range:	$12 -39	$88 -125	$125 -130		$30 -46	$50 -100	$32 -50	$12 -25

DeSantis makes and sells virtually every variety of holster described in this book. Prices are very reasonable, and quality is high. Also sells dress belts, magazine carriers, portfolios, etc. DeSantis holsters provide a great deal of "bang for the buck."

Dillon Precision 8009 E. Dillons Way Scottsdale, AZ 85260 (800) 223-4570	IWB	Shoulder	Purse	Women's	Ankle	Fanny Pack	Scabbard	Pocket
Price Range:								

Carries concealment products from several makers including Bianchi and Kramer. Also sells the Dillon line of economical holsters. Sells a wide range of shooting supplies and accessories.

Doctor Center 4244 Maine Ave. Dept. F Baldwin Park, CA 91706 (800) 442-3627	IWB	Shoulder	Purse	Women's	Ankle	Fanny Pack	Scabbard	Pocket
Price Range:								

Sells the "Conceal It secret gunbelt". Basically, it's a bellyband-style belt that can be worn low on the belly or higher up, around the chest (there's an over-the-shoulder strap to help hold it up). Unit has a cloth-backed pad under the gun to help keep the gun off your skin. Comes in a variety of sizes for $29.

Eagle Grips 460 Randy Rd. Carol Stream, IL 60188 (800) 323-6144 Catalog $1	IWB	Shoulder	Purse	Women's	Ankle	Fanny Pack	Scabbard	Pocket
Price Range:								

Sells wooden replacement grips for popular revolvers that are designed for concealment.

Eagle Industries Unlimited 400 Biltmore Drive, Suite 530 Fenton, MO 63026 (314) 343-7547	IWB	Shoulder	Purse	Women's	Ankle	Fanny Pack	Scabbard	Pocket
Price Range:	$14 -19	$30 -60			$25 -35	$55		

Eagle sells nylon holsters and other accessories. If you are looking for a shoulder holster for a submachine gun, they have one.

El Paso Saddlery, Co. P.O. Box 27194 El Paso, TX 79926 (915) 544-2233 Catalog $3	*IWB*	*Shoulder*	*Purse*	*Women's*	*Ankle*	*Fanny Pack*	*Scabbard*	*Pocket*
Price Range:		$85 -90					$45 -60	

Hand-made leather goods since 1889. Sells lots of "cowboy style" reproductions, and a few concealment items.

Feminine Protection, Inc. 10514 Shady Trail Dallas, TX 75220 (800)444-7090	*IWB*	*Shoulder*	*Purse*	*Women's*	*Ankle*	*Fanny Pack*	*Scabbard*	*Pocket*
Price Range:			$50 -195	$50		$30 -50		$20

Sells purses, bags, and portfolios with integral holsters. Purses come in over 30 styles in 10 colors and 20 sizes. Also sells a bellyband-like rig and a garter-belt holster.

J. Flores Publications P.O. Box 830131 Miami, FL 33283-0131 (800) 472-2388	*IWB*	*Shoulder*	*Purse*	*Women's*	*Ankle*	*Fanny Pack*	*Scabbard*	*Pocket*
Price Range:								

Sells a unique below-the-waistband rig called the "Defender" for $30. This consists of an elastic belt that can carry a gun and/or extra ammo.

Galati International Box 326 Catawissa, MO 63015 (314) 257-4837	*IWB*	*Shoulder*	*Purse*	*Women's*	*Ankle*	*Fanny Pack*	*Scabbard*	*Pocket*
Price Range:		$25				$20 -30		

Nylon holsters, accessories, and gun cases. Four different styles of shoulder holsters, all $25.

Galco International, Ltd. 2019 W. Quail Avenue Phoenix, AZ 85027 (602) 258-8295 Catalog $8	*IWB*	*Shoulder*	*Purse*	*Women's*	*Ankle*	*Fanny Pack*	*Scabbard*	*Pocket*
Price Range:	$19 -70	$75 -150	$225	$45 -90	$42 -62	$58 -150	$42 -80	$30 -36

A full-line dealer, Galco sells very nice holsters. Makes fitted holsters for most guns, and everything appears to be available for lefties. Home of the "Miami Classic" shoulder rig worn by Don Johnson in the "Miami Vice" series. Carries a wide selection of gun and dress belts. Catalog is full-color and 69 pages, though it's expensive. Lots of gun stores carry Galco products.

Galls, Inc. 2680 Palumbo Drive P.O. Box 54308 Lexington, KY 40555-4308 (800) 477-7766	*IWB*	*Shoulder*	*Purse*	*Women's*	*Ankle*	*Fanny Pack*	*Scabbard*	*Pocket*
Price Range:								

Resells holsters from a variety of manufacturers, including Ahern, Gould & Goodrich, Safariland, Thunderwear, and Uncle Mike's. Also sells the Spiewak "Hidden Agenda" line of jackets. They cater to the law enforcement/public safety market, but they have products of interest to all gun owners—and great service.

GML Products, Inc 394 Laredo Dr. Birmingham, AL 35226 (800) 345-2247	*IWB*	*Shoulder*	*Purse*	*Women's*	*Ankle*	*Fanny Pack*	*Scabbard*	*Pocket*
Price Range:			$90 -130					

"Protective Fashion by Gloria Le Master" sells leather holster purses and portfolios. They are available in a variety of styles and colors.

Goshen Enterprises, Inc. P.O. Box 20489 Village of Oak Creek, AZ 86341 (602) 284-1483	*IWB*	*Shoulder*	*Purse*	*Women's*	*Ankle*	*Fanny Pack*	*Scabbard*	*Pocket*
Price Range:		$200	$415 -550	$131	$125		$78 -160	

Goshen custom-makes holsters to fit *your* gun (turnaround time is about 3 weeks, write for details). Expensive, but ideal for customized weaponry. Also makes several leather belt-pouch holsters that don't look like holsters (they look like a carrier for your glasses, or tool pouches, or something other than a holster).

Gould&Goodrich 709 E. McNeil St. P.O. Box 1479 Lillington, NC 27546 (919) 893-2071	*IWB*	*Shoulder*	*Purse*	*Women's*	*Ankle*	*Fanny Pack*	*Scabbard*	*Pocket*
Price Range:	$10 -17	$56 -97		$30	$33			

Holsters and accessories, in nylon and leather models. Carries two different bellyband-type rigs, one specifically for women.

Guardian Leather, Inc. P.O. Box 277 Newton Centre, MA 02159 (800) 597-3826	*IWB*	*Shoulder*	*Purse*	*Women's*	*Ankle*	*Fanny Pack*	*Scabbard*	*Pocket*
Price Range:			$110 -140		$40	$40 -60		

Purses, bags, and portfolios with integral holsters. A level IIIa body armor insert is available for their large portfolio. Their holster purse comes with a wrist loop that fits around your handgun grip for faster access. Also sells a bellyband type rig for $20 and a holster that can be mounted under tables and such for $15.

The Gunfitters P.O. Box 426 Cambridge, WI 53523-0426 (608) 764-8128	*IWB*	*Shoulder*	*Purse*	*Women's*	*Ankle*	*Fanny Pack*	*Scabbard*	*Pocket*
Price Range:							$75 -105	$55

Handmade, custom molded leather holsters. Will work with you to design and build exactly what you want. Prices are quite reasonable for this kind of custom work.

Hafner Creations Inc. Rt. 1 Box 248A Lake City, FL 32055 (904) 755-6481	*IWB*	*Shoulder*	*Purse*	*Women's*	*Ankle*	*Fanny Pack*	*Scabbard*	*Pocket*
Price Range:	$10 -14	$16 -25			$13 -28	$16 -49	$8 -14	

Hafner makes and sells nylon holsters in a variety of styles at reasonable prices. They make holsters for guns equipped with lasers and scopes. They will also custom-make a nylon holster to your specs, for about 20% extra. Call for details. Also sells range bags and gun cases, at very affordable prices.

Hellweg Ltd. 40356 Oak Park Way, Suite H Oakhurst, CA 93644 (800) 450-1911	*IWB*	*Shoulder*	*Purse*	*Women's*	*Ankle*	*Fanny Pack*	*Scabbard*	*Pocket*
Price Range:							$79	

Hellweg sells holsters that are designed for both concealed carry *and* competition, in the theory that using only one holster maximizes the self-defense training value of competition. They also sell dress belts.

Hogue Grips P.O. Box 1138 Paso Robles, CA 93447 (800) 438-4747	IWB	Shoulder	Purse	Women's	Ankle	Fanny Pack	Scabbard	Pocket
Price Range:								

Hogue sells replacement grips in a variety of styles for most handguns.

Horseshoe Leather Products The Cottage, Sharow RIPON HG4 5BP England (0765) 605858	IWB	Shoulder	Purse	Women's	Ankle	Fanny Pack	Scabbard	Pocket
Price Range:	$38 -72	$95 -160					$50 -85	

This is Andy Arratoonian's firm. He sells handmade molded leather holsters, all of which are designed for concealment. Produces a deep concealment IWB rig that has its own belt that is worn under the pants, so that there's nothing visible on your belt. Nothing is available for lefties.

Don Hume Leathergoods P.O. Box 351 Miami, OK 74355-0351 (800) 331-2686	IWB	Shoulder	Purse	Women's	Ankle	Fanny Pack	Scabbard	Pocket
Price Range:		$59					$27 -32	

Also has belts and magazine/speedloader carriers. Few concealment products, caters primarily to the law enforcement market.

Hunter Company, Inc. 3300 West 71st Ave. P.O. Box 467 Westminster, CO 80030-9977 (303) 427-4626	IWB	Shoulder	Purse	Women's	Ankle	Fanny Pack	Scabbard	Pocket
Price Range:	$67	$67					$17 -31	

Top-grain leather holsters with thumb-breaks. Also has ammo carriers in leather and nylon.

KG Products 1740 Churchill Dr. Oakland, OR 97462 (800) 944-7717	IWB	Shoulder	Purse	Women's	Ankle	Fanny Pack	Scabbard	Pocket
Price Range:			$55 -110			$15 -65		

Sells holster purses, bags, and fannypacks in a variety of sizes, styles, and colors.

Kirkpatrick Leather Company P.O. Box 3150 Laredo, TX 78044-3150 (210) 723-6631	IWB	Shoulder	Purse	Women's	Ankle	Fanny Pack	Scabbard	Pocket
Price Range:		$70 -83					$40 -50	

Leather molded holsters, mainly for the law enforcement market.

Kramer Handgun Leather P.O. Box 112154 Tacoma, WA 98411 (206) 564-6652	IWB	Shoulder	Purse	Women's	Ankle	Fanny Pack	Scabbard	Pocket
Price Range:	$85 -100	$145		$100	$150		$85 -95	$78

A custom shop that caters to the armed professional, Kramer uses nothing but horsehide leather in their products. Kramer's motto is "A superior holster cannot be had at any price." Top-quality work, at a top-quality price. The Kramer pocket holster is one of the best available. Also sells dress belts and ammo carriers.

Lady B Safe 6120 E Admiral Place Tulsa, OK 74115-8624 (800) 627-8027	IWB	Shoulder	Purse	Women's	Ankle	Fanny Pack	Scabbard	Pocket
Price Range:			$130					

Hand-crafted leather holster purses in a variety of styles and colors. Approved for use by the Federal Marshall's Service and IRS.

LAW Concealment Systems P.O. Box 3952 Wilmington, NC 28406 (910) 791-6656	IWB	Shoulder	Purse	Women's	Ankle	Fanny Pack	Scabbard	Pocket
Price Range:	$39 -48							$39

LAW sells a line of unique IWB holster "pouches" that come in leather (rough side out) or nylon. They have a flap that extends up from the holster's "mouth" to keep the gun from touching your skin. With the larger models, the gun can be carried straight up, canted, or crossdraw. Comfortable and concealable, these holsters are an excellent choice for "hard to fit" guns. However, believe them when they say it will take a couple of months to break in the leather versions. The holster will be much more comfortable then.

The Leather Arsenal 27549 Middleton Rd. Middleton, ID 83644 (208) 585-6212	IWB	Shoulder	Purse	Women's	Ankle	Fanny Pack	Scabbard	Pocket
Price Range:	$40 -68							

Handmade cowhide concealment holsters and magazine pouches at reasonable prices. They make two IWB models, both of which have reinforced mouths and are made rough side out. One has a flap that extends upward from the holster mouth to keep the gun from touching your skin. Left handed models cost $5-$10 extra.

Leatherwood Holsters 360 Teel Rd. Winchendon, MA 01475 (508) 297-0505	IWB	Shoulder	Purse	Women's	Ankle	Fanny Pack	Scabbard	Pocket
Price Range:	$19 -80		$119		$44	$59		$24

Sells the "Hidden Difference" knife-sheath/pager case holster that carries the gun below the waistband and can be worn without a coat. Also sells the Strong "mini money wallet" to help avoid that "two wallet" look when carrying in a wallet holster.

Lincoln Leathercrafts P.O. Box 9613 Peoria, IL 61614	IWB	Shoulder	Purse	Women's	Ankle	Fanny Pack	Scabbard	Pocket
Price Range:								$40 -45

Leather pocket holsters for popular small revolvers and autos.

Love Leathers Inc. 3415 "O" St. Vancouver, WA 98663 (206) 693-3812	*IWB*	*Shoulder*	*Purse*	*Women's*	*Ankle*	*Fanny Pack*	*Scabbard*	*Pocket*
Price Range:			$65			$30 -70		

Leather fanny packs, bags, and purses with gun compartments in a variety of styles and colors.

Magnolia Sports, Inc. 211 W. Main Magnolia, AR 71753 (800) 530-7816	*IWB*	*Shoulder*	*Purse*	*Women's*	*Ankle*	*Fanny Pack*	*Scabbard*	*Pocket*
Price Range:	$10 -16	$35 -67			$35		$15 -30	

Nylon holsters and accessories, some available with or without safety straps. Several ambidextrous models are available.

Midway P.O. Box 1483 Columbia, MO 65203 (800) 243-3220	*IWB*	*Shoulder*	*Purse*	*Women's*	*Ankle*	*Fanny Pack*	*Scabbard*	*Pocket*
Price Range:								

Shooting supplies at good prices. Carries Uncle Mike's, Bianchi, and other brands of holsters. Free shipping to the first 48 states and great service. If you shoot much, you need to see their catalog.

Mika's Pocket Holsters Rt. 1 Box 1234 Readstown, WI 54652 (608) 627-1152	*IWB*	*Shoulder*	*Purse*	*Women's*	*Ankle*	*Fanny Pack*	*Scabbard*	*Pocket*
Price Range:	$24							$10

Sells inexpensive pocket holsters, with different designs for front and back pockets.

Mitchell Leatherworks 12 Mansion Rd. Dunbarton, NH 03045 (603) 774-6283	IWB	Shoulder	Purse	Women's	Ankle	Fanny Pack	Scabbard	Pocket
Price Range:	$95						$90	$46

A one-man shop, Mitchell specializes in hand-made leather holsters. Top-quality work, though not inexpensive. Will custom make a holster for any gun. Also sells dress belts and a unique magazine/flashlight carrier—the "SOS." Also sells the ARG—"Ayoob Rear Guard" designed with Massad Ayoob.

Mixson Leathercraft, Inc. 7435 West 19th Court Hialeah, FL (800) 327-0078	IWB	Shoulder	Purse	Women's	Ankle	Fanny Pack	Scabbard	Pocket
Price Range:	$10						$15 -41	

Catering to the law enforcement market, Mixson carries few concealment products. Prices shown are "police prices".

Bruce Nelson Combat Leather P.O. Box 8691 Tucson, AZ 85738 (602) 825-9047 Catalog $3	IWB	Shoulder	Purse	Women's	Ankle	Fanny Pack	Scabbard	Pocket
Price Range:	$55			$117 -127	$125		$85 -95	$59

Hand-made molded leather holsters, belts, and accessories. This catalog makes interesting reading, as it explains why BNCL products were designed the way they were. Bruce designed the classic "Summer Special" (though others are licensed to make it as well). Also sells a purse/briefcase insert for $105.

K.L. Null Holsters Ltd. Hill City Station Resaca, GA 30735 (706) 625-5643 Catalog $3	IWB	Shoulder	Purse	Women's	Ankle	Fanny Pack	Scabbard	Pocket
Price Range:	$110	$50 -55			$100 -110		$115 -125	$50

Hand-made, molded leather and synthetic holsters in a variety of styles and colors. The SPS (Side Pocket Scabbard) is an excellent pocket holster for a coat or other large pocket. They also sell the "Leech", which at $15 is a strap that wraps around your weapon and will snap on to various other items.

On Target Enterprises,Inc. P.O. Box 372 Harrisburg, NC 28075 (704) 785-9567	IWB	Shoulder	Purse	Women's	Ankle	Fanny Pack	Scabbard	Pocket
Price Range:			$50 -57			$34 -60		

Leather gun bags, fannypacks, and purses in a variety of styles and colors. Also sells the "Conceal-It" bellyband-style under-the-shirt rig for $25.

Pachmayr, Ltd. 1875 S. Mountain Ave. Monrovia, CA 91016 (818) 357-7771	IWB	Shoulder	Purse	Women's	Ankle	Fanny Pack	Scabbard	Pocket
Price Range:								$17

Pachmayr sells a variety of firearm accessories and parts. They also sell the "T.A.C. Tactical Pocket Holster". This allows pocket carry of a J-frame S&W revolver, while giving the appearance of a wallet. They also sell replacement grips for many guns.

Pistol Packaging, Inc. 765 Tower Drive Hamel, MN 55340 (800) 545-8016	IWB	Shoulder	Purse	Women's	Ankle	Fanny Pack	Scabbard	Pocket
Price Range:	$11	$45					$29	

Sells the "Tri-vertible" leather holster that can be worn as a vertical or horizontal shoulder rig, or as a belt holster. Holsters come with a lifetime guarantee.

PistolERA 5760 Corsair Court Bensalem, PA 19020 (215) 752-9131	IWB	Shoulder	Purse	Women's	Ankle	Fanny Pack	Scabbard	Pocket
Price Range:				$110 -175				

Custom-made women's apparel specifically for concealed handgun carry. Garments contain the gun in adjustable inserts.

Portfolios Plus 224 North Lansdowne Ave. Lansdowne, PA 19050 (800) 688-8173	IWB	Shoulder	Purse	Women's	Ankle	Fanny Pack	Scabbard	Pocket
Price Range:								

Sells leather portfolios with concealed gun compartments for $199.

Pro Carry Systems Int. 7818 Express St. Burnaby, BC V5A 1T4 (800) 665-7757	IWB	Shoulder	Purse	Women's	Ankle	Fanny Pack	Scabbard	Pocket
Price Range:	$25	$46				$63 -69	$40	

Nylon holsters and accessories. Their IWB holster has a flap on the inside that extends up to keep your gun from touching your skin.

PW Gun Leather P.O. Box 450432 Atlanta, GA 30345 (404) 822-1640	*IWB*	*Shoulder*	*Purse*	*Women's*	*Ankle*	*Fanny Pack*	*Scabbard*	*Pocket*
Price Range:	$20 -47	$64 -99			$75		$30 -60	

Wet molded and hand-boned leather holsters, available for most common guns. Sells a molded purse insert holster for $111 and a document pouch holster for $155. Also sells a cummerbund holster for $75, though it's not illustrated in their catalog.

Renegade Holster and Leather Co. P.O. Box 31546 Phoenix, AZ 85046 (602) 482-6777	*IWB*	*Shoulder*	*Purse*	*Women's*	*Ankle*	*Fanny Pack*	*Scabbard*	*Pocket*
Price Range:	$21 -30				$37 -41			

Sells the "Cozy Partner" line of ankle holsters, and the "Ghost" line of faired IWB holsters. The "Ghost" units can be attached to your belt or pants with Velcro, and allow your shirt to be tucked in over the gun. One of the very few holsters on the market that allows this.

Ringler Custom Leather Box 206 Cody, WY 82414 (307) 645-3255	*IWB*	*Shoulder*	*Purse*	*Women's*	*Ankle*	*Fanny Pack*	*Scabbard*	*Pocket*
Price Range:							$55 -67	

Handmade leather goods. Many "cowboy style" items, but offer a couple of concealment products in addition.

Thad Rybka Custom Leather Equipment 134 Havilah Hill St. Odenville, AL 35120 Catalog $3	IWB	Shoulder	Purse	Women's	Ankle	Fanny Pack	Scabbard	Pocket
Price Range:								$45 -50

Ambidextrous leather pocket holsters for most small guns. Also sells a pocket magazine pouch.

Safariland 3120 East Mission Blvd. Ontario, CA 91761 (800) 347-1200	IWB	Shoulder	Purse	Women's	Ankle	Fanny Pack	Scabbard	Pocket
Price Range:	$13 -44	$47 -108	$131 -250				$24 -60	

Caters primarily to the law enforcement market, but does carry some concealment products. Both nylon and leather holsters are available, along with speedloader/magazine carriers, belts, etc. Safariland products are carried by many mail-order houses and gun stores.

Second Chance Body Armor P.O. Box 578 Central Lake, MI 49622 (800) 253-7090	IWB	Shoulder	Purse	Women's	Ankle	Fanny Pack	Scabbard	Pocket
Price Range:								

While not *really* a concealment product, Second Chance sells a holster that bears mention. It's a nylon/Kevlar belt holster that is bullet-resistant. It's designed to prevent injury from accidental discharges. Cost is $130.

SeeR, Inc. P.O. Box 20983 Waco, TX 76702-0983	*IWB*	*Shoulder*	*Purse*	*Women's*	*Ankle*	*Fanny Pack*	*Scabbard*	*Pocket*
Price Range:								

Seer sells a dummy pager for $20 that will hold small derringers or .22/.25 autos.

Tex Shoemaker and Son 714 West Cienega Ave. San Dimas, CA 91773 (800) 345-9959	*IWB*	*Shoulder*	*Purse*	*Women's*	*Ankle*	*Fanny Pack*	*Scabbard*	*Pocket*
Price Range:	$13 -21	$90 -170			$51		$44	$25

Leather holster maker that caters primarily to the law enforcement market.   Carries belt holsters for guns with laser sights, and magazine and speedloader carriers.

Shooting Systems Group 1075 Headquarters Park Fenton, MO 63026-2478 (800) 325-3049	*IWB*	*Shoulder*	*Purse*	*Women's*	*Ankle*	*Fanny Pack*	*Scabbard*	*Pocket*
Price Range:	$19 -25	$44 -87			$35	$45	$35	

Sells nylon holsters and accessories. Some of their holsters feature a molded sight track, to cut down on snagging during the draw. Most of their holsters use plastic and/or metal for support or strength, where appropriate. If you like polymer or composite holsters, check these folks out.

Milt Sparks Holsters, Inc. 605 East 44th, #2 Boise, Idaho 83714 (208) 377-5577	IWB	Shoulder	Purse	Women's	Ankle	Fanny Pack	Scabbard	Pocket
Price Range:	$42 -65				$85		$62 -65	$35

Milt Sparks specializes in top-quality molded leather holsters, available for most guns and in left or right handed. Noted gun writer and former IPSC world champion Ross Seyfried considers Milt Sparks holsters to be the best in the world. Their "Executives Companion" and "Summer Special" IWB holsters are some of the best we've tried. Also sells belts and ammo carriers. Moderately priced products, and a great value.

I. Spiewak 505 Eighth Ave. New York, NY 10018 (800) 223-6850	IWB	Shoulder	Purse	Women's	Ankle	Fanny Pack	Scabbard	Pocket
Price Range:								

Sells the "Hidden Agenda" line of jackets. Available in several styles, with retail prices starting around $90.

Strong Holster Company 105 Maplewood Ave. Gloucester, MA 01930 (508) 281-3300 Catalog $3	IWB	Shoulder	Purse	Women's	Ankle	Fanny Pack	Scabbard	Pocket
Price Range:	$10 -16	$40 -140					$40 -55	$19

Strong carries a variety of leather and nylon holsters for duty use or concealed carry. Notable among their line is the "Piecekeeper" scabbard holster with a clever retention device. They also sell a bellyband type rig, as well as mag carriers, dress belts, and the like.

Tabler Marketing 2554 Lincoln Blvd. #555 Marina Del Rey, CA 90291 (818) 366-7485	IWB	Shoulder	Purse	Women's	Ankle	Fanny Pack	Scabbard	Pocket
Price Range:								

Sells the "Cincher" adjustable belt-slide holster. Adjusts to carry everything from small autos through big guns like Desert Eagles and M-11s. It's ambidextrous, will fit guns with scopes, and contacts the gun with a sheepskin pad. Available in a variety of colors and finishes. Prices range from $30 to $100.

Tactical Edge 4790 Clover Meadows Dr. Meridian, ID 83642 (208) 327-0217	IWB	Shoulder	Purse	Women's	Ankle	Fanny Pack	Scabbard	Pocket
Price Range:						$35		

Sells nylon fanny packs, range bags, and police equipment organizers. Also has advertised a day-planner holster, though pricing was not available at press time.

Tauris Holsters 3695 Mohawk St. New Hartford, NY 13413 (315) 737-9115	IWB	Shoulder	Purse	Women's	Ankle	Fanny Pack	Scabbard	Pocket
Price Range:	$50	$60 -90			$60 -70		$45 -50	

Custom-made leather holsters and accessories at reasonable prices. Available in a variety of colors and finishes, and in both left and right-handed models.

Thunderwear, Inc. P.O. Box 372460 Satellite Beach, FL 32937 (800) 375-4433	IWB	Shoulder	Purse	Women's	Ankle	Fanny Pack	Scabbard	Pocket
Price Range:								

Sells the Thunderwear beneath-the-waistline holsters for $45. They are available in black or white and in sizes to fit small or medium handguns.

Uncle Mike's P.O. Box 13010 Portland, OR 97213 (505) 255-6890	IWB	Shoulder	Purse	Women's	Ankle	Fanny Pack	Scabbard	Pocket
Price Range:	$11 -17	$35 -50			$34	$27 -42	$19 -24	$8

Nylon holsters and accessories. Sells hip and shoulder holsters for guns with lasers or scopes. Sells a mesh belly-band rig with perspiration-proof holster for $35. Uncle Mike's products are available from many sporting goods stores and mail-order houses.

U.S. Cavalry 2855 Centennial Ave. Radcliff, KY 40160-9000 (800) 777-7732	IWB	Shoulder	Purse	Women's	Ankle	Fanny Pack	Scabbard	Pocket
Price Range:								

U.S. Cavalry is a reseller of various brands of holsters, including Thunderwear, DeSantis, and Bianchi. They sell quite a few self-defense related items, and a variety of other products that are useful to the gunowner.

FOR INFORMATION
About Ordering This Book, Please Write:

B&R Company
2800 Old Dawson Road
Suite 2, Box 206
Albany, GA 31707

A volume price list is available upon request.